Moses

Steps to a Life of Faith

Bob Saffrin

Bob Saffrin

Scriptures taken from the Holy Bible, New International Version®, NIV®. Copyright © 1973, 1978, 1984, 2011 by Biblica, Inc.™ Used by permission of Zondervan. All rights reserved worldwide. www.zondervan.com.

The "NIV" and "New International Version" are trademarks registered in the United States Patent and Trademark Office by Biblica, Inc.™

Cover image used by license agreement Waj111, Dreamstime LLC

ACKNOWLEDGMENTS

Thanks so much to my wife Barb for her great editing skills and to Joy Christiansen for her terrific cover design. I also want to thank Rocky for not barking too much while I was trying to write the manuscript.

PREFACE

God is a dreamer. One day he had a dream and then he thought to himself, "Who will I get to live my dream?" And then he made you. He created you to fulfill a dream. You are made for a purpose. This book is about knowing God's dream for your life and believing him to accomplish it in you. This could be the most exciting thing that has ever happened to you. To enter into God's plan for your life is to become the person he made you to be and to finally find the fulfillment and joy that you have been seeking your whole life.

If you know Jesus as your Savior, then this book can help bring you to the next level of your walk with him. If you don't know God and have never asked him into your life, then this book won't be much help in finding his plan for you. You really can't fulfill the dream of someone you don't know. There is good news though. It turns out that God himself wants you to know him. He made you primarily because he wants to have a relationship with you. Actually, God loves you so much that 2000 years ago he sent his only son to earth to pay the penalty for your sins, just so he can have a relationship with you. God is holy and can't have a relationship with anyone who has sin in their life, and the Bible says that we have all sinned. There would be no hope for any of us except that Jesus paid the penalty for our sin so that we can stand sinless before a holy God. Many people think they have to clean up their act before God will accept them; this is just not true. God will take you just the way you are, warts and all. All God requires of us is to "want" him in our life and "accept" his sacrifice for us.

This sounds complicated but it really isn't. God will instantly begin to work in your life through a simple, heartfelt prayer. Keep in mind that I'm not talking about religion; all religions are about man trying to reach to God.   I'm not talking about that. God is reaching to you today because he wants to know you and have a relationship with you. If you are ready now to receive Jesus into your life, you can pray the simple prayer below from your heart and you will instantly become part of God's family. If you aren't sure if you are ready, that's okay. Read this book, and as God's Spirit begins to stir in you, you can come back here anytime and pray the prayer.

Prayer to receive Jesus:

"Dear God,

I'm a sinner. I'm sorry for my sins and want to turn away from them. I believe that you, Jesus Christ, are the son of God. I believe that you died for me, that you rose from the grave, and that you are alive. I invite you right now to come into my heart to take control. By faith I receive you into my heart to be my God, my friend, my savior, and my Lord. I pray this in the name of Jesus.

Amen"

PROLOGUE

Many years ago when I first started studying the Bible, I pretty much stayed in the New Testament. Even though there was a lot I didn't understand, there was also a lot that was just easy to take at face value. By contrast, the Old Testament was pretty much a mystery to me. As I studied more and more, and the Holy Spirit began opening the whole book to me, I started to understand why the Lord gave us the Old Testament. First of all, the Lord's heart is revealed in the Old Testament like nowhere else. In the Old Testament we see Jehovah dealing with an often rebellious nation of Israel and how he never gave up on them in spite of how badly they treated him. The Old Testament gives us huge revelation into the heart of God. Secondly, the Old Testament gives us great stories that model the doctrines of the New Testament.

What the New Testament states, the Old Testament illustrates.

I've come to love the Old Testament stories. In particular, I love the little biblical biographies like David and Esther and Elijah, and many others. I love it when Jehovah takes just ordinary people and uses them to accomplish mighty things for the Kingdom of God.

I love superhero stories. As a kid I loved to watch superman on TV. I love to watch action movies because I can imagine myself in the place of the heroes. Through their stories I can have great adventures and do mighty deeds. It is fun, but it is, of course, all imaginary. But the Bible is real. All of the stories are true, and yet each story is better than any movie you will watch or any book that you will read. However, there is a difference. The men and women in the Bible aren't really heroes. David wasn't a hero, he was a sinner. Apart from God, Elijah was a coward. Abraham was a liar. Jacob was a deceiver. You will find none of the so-called Bible heroes to be true heroes. They were just ordinary sinners like you and me. There is only one true hero in the Bible. Jehovah is the hero of every Bible story.

Now here is the wonderful part. When you read an adventure story or see a movie, in your imagination you put yourself in the place of the hero and pretend that you can do the things that he or she can do. But the Bible stories are different. None of the Bible characters were up to the adventures they found themselves in. None were capable enough. None were worthy. None were courageous enough. They were just people like you and me who found a way to connect with and tap into the power of the living God. None of the Bible characters had what it takes to be a hero. The mystery is that because these were just ordinary people like you and me, we all have the potential to have great adventures with Jehovah just like they did. Because all of the power rests in God and none in me, I don't have to be good enough or capable enough or courageous enough.

A few years ago I was in India teaching on the life of Moses at a conference for pastors and leaders. I told the attendees that God had an "A" plan for each of their lives, and that his "A" plan for them was just as big as the plan he had for Moses. I told them that God is not a God of small dreams and that each of them could have a ministry that was no less important in the kingdom of God than was the ministry that God gave Moses. The question is not how big is God, but rather, how much can we believe

9

him. During a break at the conference, a young lady asked if she could speak with me. We went out into the center of a vacant lot to talk. She began to cry. She said, "All my life, starting with my parents, people have been telling me that my life would never amount to anything. Now I come to this seminar and you tell me that God has a dream for my life that is just as big as the dream he had for Moses. How can this be?" I explained to her that the size of God's dream for her life isn't dependent on what others thought, or her worthiness, her talent, or even her faithfulness, but rather is dependent wholly on God. I assured her that God is big enough to have a huge dream for every person on the planet. I explained that there isn't anything that Moses did or who he was that is beyond our ability, because all of our ability rests in God. I have come to know this young lady personally, even though I have not seen her for several years now. She has several college degrees and is married to a great young pastor. I trust God is using her in a mighty way.

This book is going to focus on the story of Moses and his journey with God to become the man that God made him to be and to live the dream that God dreamed for him. One valid question we can ask about all of the so-called Bible heroes is -"Why them?" Why did God choose them to do great and mighty things for the kingdom? Was there something that all the great men and women of the Bible had in common that made them so usable by God?

I believe there was one thing; one common thread that weaves itself through all the stories of the great Bible characters. All of them had great faith. All of them were available to God; all of them believed him for what he could do with their lives. They didn't all start with great faith, but each of them had that bent toward believing that allowed God to build great faith into their lives.

And so, as we explore Moses' story together, I want us to discover what faith really is; to watch it work its way through Moses' life. I'm praying that faith will rise in our hearts as we take the next step in the great adventure that Jesus has for each of us. *By faith Moses, when he had grown up, refused to be known as the son of Pharaoh's daughter. He chose to be mistreated along with the people of God rather than to enjoy the pleasures of sin for a short time. He regarded disgrace for the sake of Christ as of greater value than the treasures of Egypt, because he was looking ahead to his reward (Heb 11:24-26).*

As I've studied Moses' life and witnessed what God was able to do with one flawed man, my faith has grown. As you read this book, my prayer is that yours will as well.

CHAPTER 1

Faith…Does God Give it to me…or
Do I Need To Come Up With It On My Own

Faith is one of those words that we Christians use liberally, and yet we often find difficult to adequately define in a meaningful way. Let's consider the concept of faith before we dive into looking at Moses' story, because Moses' story is a story of how God built faith into a man.

So, what really is faith?

The Oxford dictionary defines faith as "complete trust or confidence in someone or something." So if we are talking about Christian faith, that would be complete trust and confidence in God. The difficulty for most people is with that word "complete." We struggle to trust God completely. But over and over in the Bible we are told that God is a God who above all wants us to trust him with everything. Actually that is what we want too. God has created us with a need to be able to completely trust someone. Everyone on the planet is yearning for someone to believe in; it's wired into our DNA. Unfortunately, most people have tried trust with another person and been let down. We will always let each other down because we are all mortal and flawed. Many have come to the conclusion that they can't trust anyone or that they just need to look out for themselves. That conclusion can only lead to an unsuccessful and unhappy life. Only God can satisfy that built-in need we all have to completely trust someone.

What is the source of faith?

Is faith something we are just supposed to gen up in ourselves, or does God supply faith? If God supplies faith, then does that make it his fault when we lack faith? Maybe you have never even asked these questions, but they have haunted me at various times in my life. As a student of God's Word, I have sought answers, but found that even what the Bible offers can appear to be confusing and contradictory.

This may seem like a simple question, but it has long been the source of much Christian controversy. I remember a story I heard about a pastor who preached that if you have enough faith, whatever you ask for will be given to you. Whenever someone in the church would get sick, he would go to them and tell them that they had to have more faith if they wanted to get well. One day the pastor got sick with a serious illness. The church people all came to visit him in the hospital to ask if he was sick because he had some sin in his life, or because he didn't have enough faith to be healed. It wasn't very encouraging for this suffering man. It took him a long time before he was well and by that time he had become so discouraged he quit the ministry, feeling that God no longer cared for him.

So the question remains. Are we supposed to just grit our teeth and believe, or does God somehow supply it for us? As always, we look to God's Word when we need answers. What does the Bible say about faith? Look at 2 Peter 1:1: *Simon Peter, a servant and apostle of Jesus Christ, to those who through the righteousness of our God and Savior Jesus Christ have received a faith as precious as ours.*

We've all heard it said, "You have to have faith if you want God's blessing on your life." 2 Peter 1:1 says

15

that we receive faith through the righteousness of Jesus. In fact, look at 2 Peter 1:3: *His divine power has given us everything we need for life and godliness through our knowledge of him who called us by his own glory and goodness.* Peter tells us that God has given us everything we need. I guess that would include faith. But wait! Remember the story about the Roman centurion who brought his son to Jesus to be healed? Jesus would have gone to the man's house to heal his son, but the centurion replied, *"Lord, I do not deserve to have you come under my roof. But just say the word, and my servant will be healed" (Matt 8:8).* Jesus' response to the soldier was that he was astonished and said, *"I tell you the truth, I have not found anyone in Israel with such great faith (Matt 8:10).* Did the Centurion have faith within him or did God give him the faith? If God gave him the faith, why was Jesus astonished? Which is correct? Is faith something we're supposed to have or something we're supposed to get? Go down just a few verses to Matt 8:23-26: *Then he (Jesus) got into the boat and his disciples followed him. Without warning, a furious storm came up on the lake, so that the waves swept over the boat. But Jesus was sleeping. The disciples went and woke him, saying, "Lord, save us! We're going to drown!" He replied, "You of little faith, why are you so afraid?"* If God gives faith, then why would he rebuke the disciples for not having it? Then there is the story in Matt 9 of the woman who had been sick and bleeding for 12 years. She came to Jesus to be healed, and after healing her he said, *"Take heart, daughter, your faith has healed you…"* In the next chapter of Matthew (Matt 9) Jesus healed two blind men and he told them, *"According to your faith will it be done to you."* Are you confused yet?

All of these examples from Scripture tell us that we are to come up with the faith if we are to be blessed, but this seems so contradictory to 2 Peter where Peter tells us that we have received not only faith, but everything we need from God. So, what is the answer? Is faith up to us or does God provide it? The answer is "both." We have our part to do and God has his. Our part is simply to seek relationship with him. As our relationship with him grows, he builds faith into our lives.

Trusting God is the fruit of knowing him.

When you are sick or there is another crisis in your life, there are Biblical steps to faith. First pray and tell Jesus that you trust him in this circumstance. Then ask him to reveal his purpose for the circumstance and believe him to either release you from it or be with you in it. God gives us everything we need, but

17

it is up to us to decide what we will believe, what we will trust God for, and what we will choose to focus our lives on. That's why scripture says we only need a small mustard seed of faith. If we are simply inclined to believe God, he will build on that starter faith and we can become faith giants without limits. He creates it in us. Today I choose to believe God. Will you join me? *For in Christ Jesus neither circumcision nor un-circumcision has any value. The only thing that counts is faith expressing itself through love (Gal 5:6).* Faith is the only thing that counts.

CHAPTER 2

Living the Promise!

Look at 2 Peter 1:3-4: *His divine power has given us everything we need for life and godliness through our knowledge of him who called us by his own glory and goodness. Through these he has given us his very great and precious promises, so that through them you may participate in the divine nature and escape the corruption in the world caused by evil desires.*

We've already looked at verse three…God gives us everything we need. I believe verse 4 is the key to the questions we have about faith - *"through our knowledge of him."* First we have to know him. We need to have the revelation of who God is, how he feels about us, and what kind of a relationship he wants with us. We have to know how much he loves us, what he has given up so that we might live, and how he is committed to taking care of us. The scripture says: *"he has given us his very great and precious promises."* What promises? God gives us two kinds of promises. There are the promises in his word. Promises like, *"Nothing can separate you from my love."* Promises like, "*I will never leave you nor forsake you."* These are base-line promises. God has spoken them and you can take them to the bank. But God will give you more promises than are in his word. You see just like the people in the Bible, God has a very personal and unique plan for your life. He made you with a specific purpose and plan. Ask him and he will birth his plans in your heart.

And when God births his plans in your heart, the obstacles will come. We often think that when crisis comes into our lives somehow God let it happen or he wasn't paying attention. Actually, crisis is a symptom of God working in your life. Satan would leave you alone if God was ignoring you. The obstacles aren't meant to stop you. They are meant to remind you that it's his plan, not yours. The obstacles may seem too hard for you, but they're not too hard for God. The obstacles that come into your life will serve to build faith if you trust God with your circumstances.

The lesson I'm learning is that I need to keep asking Jesus to birth his plans in my heart. Then I need to learn to enjoy the ride, knowing that what he births he brings to fulfillment. I need to learn that I can believe what God births. That is the key to a mustard seed of faith. With passion, ask God to birth his plan for you. When he does, believe that what he births he will bring to fulfillment.

Noah had God's vision and passion so infused in his heart that he worked tirelessly for 120 years while everyone laughed at him. On Mount Moriah, Abraham risked all that he had and all that he was because he trusted God with the vision God had given him. Caleb proved to be a great man of faith because the vision of the promise was bigger than the giants. The three men in the fiery furnace had courage beyond themselves because their faith in the one true God was bigger than their fear of men. Jesus endured the cross for the hope set before him. Faith isn't trusting God with your dreams.

Faith is trusting God for his dreams as he births them in your heart.

Pause here and pray. Ask Jesus to birth his dreams in your heart, then believe Him and enjoy the adventure in faith. I'll make an outrageous claim for your life. You can have a dream and a life just as big and exciting as Moses. You might say, "Hold on a minute, Bob. You aren't telling me that I can be like Moses. He was such a great leader, filled with wisdom. Look at me. My life isn't even consistent. My life is filled with contrasts." Maybe you love to pray but you struggle with relationships. Maybe you have a great family, but then there's Uncle Charlie. Most of us would say that our lives are a mix, filled with successes and failures, good luck and bad, relationships that work and those that are disasters, great times with God along with other times when he seems so far away. So, you have inconsistencies in your life and your life isn't perfect. Can you still be greatly used by God? As we will see, the life of Moses presents a series of striking contrasts.

He was the child of a slave and the son of a queen.
He was born in a hut and lived in a palace.
He inherited poverty but lived in unlimited wealth.
He was the leader of armies and the keeper of flocks.
He was called the mightiest of warriors and the meekest of men.
He was educated in Pharaoh's court and lived in the desert.
He was a city boy who wandered in the wilderness.
He was backward in speech and he spoke for God.

He was the giver of the law and a picture of the grace to come.

His life illustrates huge failures of faith and unbelievable successes. His life was filled with contradictions just like yours and mine. Believe God today. He has a great dream for your life. Ask him to reveal his next step for you and then go hard after it.

CHAPTER 3

———————————

Moses – The Beginning
A New Administration (change isn't always good)

The story of Moses starts in Exodus chapter 1. The story was written by Moses himself. It begins sometime after the death of Joseph.

Then a new king, who did not know about Joseph, came to power in Egypt. "Look," he said to his people, "the Israelites have become much too numerous for us. Come, we must deal shrewdly with them or they will become even more numerous and, if war breaks out, will join our enemies, fight against us and leave the country." So they put slave masters over them to oppress them with forced labor, and they built Pithom and Rameses as store cities for Pharaoh. But the more they were oppressed, the more they multiplied and spread; so the Egyptians came to dread the Israelites and worked them ruthlessly. They made their lives bitter with hard labor in brick and mortar and with all kinds of work in the fields; in all their hard labor the Egyptians used them ruthlessly. The king of Egypt said to the Hebrew midwives, whose names were Shiphrah and Puah, "When you help the Hebrew women in childbirth and observe them on the delivery stool, if it is a boy, kill him; but if it is a girl, let her live." The midwives, however, feared God and did not do what the king of Egypt had told them to do; they let the boys live. Then the king of Egypt summoned the midwives and asked them, "Why have you done this? Why have you let the boys live?" The midwives answered Pharaoh, "Hebrew women are not like Egyptian women; they are vigorous and give birth before the midwives arrive." So God was kind to the midwives and the people increased and became even more numerous. And because the midwives feared God, he gave them families of their own. Then Pharaoh gave this order to all his people: "Every boy that is born you must throw into the Nile, but let every girl live" (Ex 1:8-22).

It's with this backdrop that Moses is born:

Now a man of the house of Levi married a Levite woman, and she became pregnant and gave birth to a son. When she saw that he was a fine child, she hid him for three months. But when she could hide him no longer, she got a papyrus basket for him and coated it with tar and pitch. Then she placed the child in it and put it among the reeds along the bank of the Nile. His sister stood at a distance to see what would happen to him. Then Pharaoh's daughter went down to the Nile to bathe, and her attendants were walking along the river bank. She saw the basket among the reeds and sent her slave girl to get it. She opened it and saw the baby. He was crying, and she felt sorry for him. "This is one of the Hebrew babies," she said. Then his sister asked Pharaoh's daughter, "Shall I go and get one of the Hebrew women to nurse the baby for you?" "Yes, go," she answered. And the girl went and got the baby's mother. Pharaoh's daughter said to her, "Take this baby and nurse him for me, and I will pay you." So the woman took the baby and nursed him. When the child grew older, she took him to Pharaoh's daughter and he became her son. She named him Moses, saying, "I drew him out of the water" (Ex 2:1-10).

There is a lot that went on here. Moses' father's name was Amram. He was a grandson of Levi, a great grandson of Jacob. According to Josephus, the Jewish historian, Amram was a Godly man who loved the nation of Israel (*Antiquities of the Jews, Book Two, Chapter 9*). Josephus records that Amram was worried about what would happen to Israel because Pharaoh had decreed that all the male babies would be put to death. Amram prayed and asked God for a savior for his people. Jehovah responded by giving Amram a dream that he would have a son and that his son would be hidden from Pharaoh. In that dream he was brought up in a surprising way to deliver his people from bondage. Amram believed God. I wonder if faith is something that can be passed from father to son...from parent to child. I wonder if growing up in a home where faith was evident was a genesis of faith for Moses.

By faith Moses' parents hid him for three months after he was born, because they saw he was no ordinary child, and they were not afraid of the king's edict (Heb 11:23). If Moses' parents were not afraid of Pharaoh, why after three months did they abandon him to the Nile? According to Josephus, rather than depending on his own ability to conceal Moses, Amram decided to depend instead on the dream that God had given him; thus, he didn't abandon Moses to the Nile but rather to the care of God. Wow! Can you imagine that? I'm more convinced than ever that the seed of Moses' faith began with his parents."

Moses' mother's name was Jacobed. The scripture says that "when she saw that he was a fine child" she hid him. Don't misunderstand her here. This doesn't mean that if Moses had a wart or something that she would have pitched him in the Nile. The word translated "fine" means that he was good in the broadest possible sense of the word. God had given Amram a dream that he and Jacobed would have a very special child that God would use to redeem his people from slavery. Amram and Jacobed believed God for that dream; when Moses was born, they could tell right away that God had delivered on his promise. God had delivered the goods.

The Israelites were in a bad way spiritually when Moses came on the scene. Many had turned to idolatry during their 400-year stay in Egypt. *On that day I swore to them that I would bring them out of Egypt into a land I had searched out for them, a land flowing with milk and honey, the most beautiful of all lands. And I said to them, "Each of you, get rid of the vile images you have set your eyes on, and do not defile yourselves with the idols of Egypt. I am the LORD your God." But they rebelled against me and would not listen to me; they did not get rid of the vile images they had set their eyes on, nor did they forsake the idols of Egypt. So I said I would pour out my wrath on them and spend my anger against them in Egypt (Ezek 20:6-8).* But there were some Israelites, like Moses' parents, who stayed true to God. As Jews, they would have been familiar with God's words to Abraham: *"...Know for certain that your descendants will be strangers in a country not their own, and they will be enslaved and mistreated four hundred years" (Genesis 15:13).* They would also have been familiar with God's promise that followed: *But I will punish the nation they serve as slaves, and afterward they will come out with great possessions. You, however, will go to your fathers in peace and be buried at a good old age. In the fourth generation your descendants will come back here, for the sin of the Amorites has not yet reached its full measure (Genesis 15:14-16).*

Let's take one more look at Moses' parents before we leave them. Amram and Jacobed were virtually unknown members of a group of slaves. They were nobodies, and even today they are not well known; and yet, they ranked among the great heroes of faith in Hebrews Chapter 11. What can we discover about faith from Moses' parents? I believe they exhibited five characteristics of genuine faith.

First of all, faith requires God to reveal himself. This has to come first, simply because you cannot have faith in someone you don't know, and you can only know God as he reveals himself to you. For Moses' parents, God revealed himself in the form of a dream to Amram. God will reveal himself to you today. He created you to have fellowship with him forever. He is not hiding. He wants to be known by you. Seek him today and he will reveal himself to you.

Second, faith sees. Hebrews 11:23 says that Moses' parents "saw that he was no ordinary child." What do you think they saw? Why is it necessary for faith to see? I thought faith was about the unseen. Actually, I don't think there was anything physical about Moses that was special. What did they see? I think they saw with the eyes of their heart. They saw in Moses what others couldn't see. They saw God's sovereign purpose for this baby. Those who have faith see what others do not see. One of the characteristics that all great Bible people of faith seem to share is the ability to see God in a situation. Remember Jehoshaphat's prayer when the Israelites were faced with an advancing enemy far superior in numbers to his own army: *"O our God, will you not judge them? For we have no power to face this vast army that is attacking us. We do not know what to do, but our eyes are upon you" (2 Chron 20:12).*

The third characteristic of faith is action. Faith must have feet. This one may be the one we as the church understand the least. In the church we seem to have adopted the sense that a good work ethic somehow contributes to our holiness. Some of us have grown up in families where our worth was subtly attached to how hard we worked. After all, faith without works is dead faith. Better get busy! I want you to hear that the action that accompanies faith has nothing to do with your works or getting busy. First of all, the works aren't our works, they are God's works. God is sovereign, he has a plan, and he is in the business of working out his plan. Faith characteristic #2 was "see." Faith sees the plan of God and then says, "Hey, I'd like a piece of the action." When by faith you see God working, then it just follows that by faith you will start to take steps toward God's plan. Moses' parents saw God working and so they went into action. They hid the baby from Pharaoh because they saw God's plan for him.

The fourth characteristic of faith is courage. *By faith Moses' parents hid him for three months after he was born, because they saw he was no ordinary child, and they were not afraid of the king's edict (Heb 11:23).* Why weren't they afraid? Wouldn't you be afraid if it were your child? They weren't afraid because they believed God for his plan.

Fear melts away in the face of faith.

The fifth characteristic of faith is risk; faith risks. Pharaoh had passed an edict that all male babies were to be put to death. If they were to preserve his life, Moses' parents would have to take risks. First they had to hide him for three months. Then they had to take the ultimate risk - they had to totally abandon Moses to the care of Jehovah. To put Moses in that basket and place it in the Nile River was the ultimate act of trust in the plan of God. When Moses' parents gave him up then God began to work. By faith they laid hold of God's sovereign plan. The Apostle Paul understood this: *I know whom I have believed, and am convinced that he is able to guard what I have entrusted to him for that day (2 Tim 1:12).* True faith involves risk. Faith starts with God revealing his plan. When you see him working, you begin to take action as you move in the same direction as God. As your growing faith melts away fear you take a leap into the unknown.

True faith launches you into the danger zone between who you are now and who God wants you to become.

Ask yourself what you are involved in that is beyond your own abilities. What are you doing outside of your comfort zone? Join the great adventure. Ask

God to reveal part of his sovereign plan to you; the part designed for you. Then as you see him working, begin to take steps with him. As you launch out you will enter the most exciting time of your life. Want to be a man or a woman of God with a big plan and a great cause? The formula is in Ps 37: *Commit your way to the LORD; trust in him and he will do this: he will make your righteousness shine like the dawn, the justice of your cause like the noonday sun (Ps 37:5-6).*

CHAPTER 4

The Child of a Slave…The Son of a Queen

When God answered the prayers of Moses' parents, he revealed how his ways are higher than our ways. God made foolishness of man's wisdom. As we've read, when the Israelites began to increase in numbers in Egypt, Pharaoh got concerned. *"O come, we must deal shrewdly with them or they will become even more numerous and, if war breaks out, will join our enemies, fight against us and leave the country" (Ex 1:10).*

Pharaoh's plan was to be shrewd and outflank the Israelites. They were already slaves and oppressed, but he was worried because they were growing in numbers far faster than the Egyptians. God had blessed the Jews as part of his promise to Abraham, that his descendants would be numbered as the sands of the seashore. Pharaoh was afraid that someday they would be a force against him. The best plan that Pharaoh could come up with was to put all the male babies to death. But God worked in such a way as to reveal the foolishness of Pharaoh's wisest plan. Pharaoh ended up paying room and board and education for the man who was to accomplish the exact thing that Pharaoh was trying to prevent. *He catches the wise in their craftiness, and the schemes of the wily are swept away (Job 5:13).* If God has hobbies, I think one of his favorites is to take the things that the world considers wise and show them to be foolish and vice versa. *Brothers, think of what you were when you were called. Not many of you were wise by human standards; not many were influential; not many were of noble birth. But God chose the foolish things of the world to shame the wise; God chose the weak things of the world to shame the strong. He chose the lowly things of this world and the despised things-and the things that are not--to nullify the things that are (1 Cor 1:26-28).* Why does God work this way? *so that no one may boast before him (Verse 29).* You see God is in the business of humbling those who exalt themselves and exalting those who humble themselves. This is one of those lessons we tend to have to learn over and over again. If you think very much about it and if you are like most, you will find that much of what you do is to gain the approval of others. As you try to "look good" to people, God humbles you because he wants you to look to him for validation, not to others. Try humbling yourself and see if God will lift you up.

As Moses was born, the 400 year period that God had ordained for the Jews to be in Egypt was drawing to an end. Moses was of the fourth generation. God had revealed to Moses' parents that he would be God's sovereign choice to lead the people out of bondage. Question? Why didn't God choose Aaron? He was Moses' older brother, a godly man, a better speaker than Moses, a more logical choice? (Apparently, God doesn't make his choices based on human logic – an important lesson for us to learn.)

Now a man of the house of Levi married a Levite woman, and she became pregnant and gave birth to a son. When she saw that he was a fine child, she hid him for three months. But when she could hide him no longer, she got a papyrus basket for him and coated it with tar and pitch. Then she placed the child in it and put it among the reeds along the bank of the

Nile. His sister stood at a distance to see what would happen to him. Then Pharaoh's daughter went down to the Nile to bathe, and her attendants were walking along the river bank. She saw the basket among the reeds and sent her slave girl to get it. She opened it and saw the baby. He was crying, and she felt sorry for him. "This is one of the Hebrew babies," she said. Then his sister asked Pharaoh's daughter, "Shall I go and get one of the Hebrew women to nurse the baby for you?" "Yes, go," she answered. And the girl went and got the baby's mother. Pharaoh's daughter said to her, "Take this baby and nurse him for me, and I will pay you." So the woman took the baby and nursed him. When the child grew older, she took him to Pharaoh's daughter and he became her son. She named him Moses, saying, "I drew him out of the water" (Ex 2:1-10).

And so Moses is saved from death and even allowed to live with his birth parents for a time. By the way, when you live a life of faith, God will often bless you and enrich you in unexpected ways. Note that Pharaoh's daughter is paying Jacobed to nurse her own child. How cool is that? It's not known how long Moses stayed with his parents but it could have been as long as 10-12 years. What things do you think Moses may have learned from his parents during those years? They would have lived out their faith in

Jehovah right in front of Moses. Moses would have heard over and over again the story of Amram's dream and that Moses was God's chosen savior for the Jewish people. Eventually, the time came for Moses to be given up to the daughter of Pharaoh. *When the child grew older, she took him to Pharaoh's daughter and he became her son. She named him Moses, saying, "I drew him out of the water" (Ex 2:10).*

She named him Moses. Some understanding of the historical setting may help us better understand the significance of these events. At that time, the queen was the rightful heir to the throne. The king only held power because he was married to the queen. The king and queen had no sons but they did have one daughter, Moses' adoptive mother. The princess was in line for the throne but only men could be Pharaoh and so the princess had to have a son to continue the royal line. The king was not in good health and the princess was very young, probably pre-teen. Who would next rule Egypt? It's in that context that the princess found Moses along the bank of the Nile. The queen might have even been involved in adopting Moses in order to provide a future heir to the throne.

And so, the day came when Moses entered the royal court for the purpose of being trained and eventually to become Pharaoh. Stephen (the disciple of Jesus) tells the story in his sermon in Acts 7: *When he was placed outside, Pharaoh's daughter took him and brought him up as her own son. Moses was educated in all the wisdom of the Egyptians and was powerful in speech and action (Acts 7:21-22).* Do you think it was a good thing that Moses was educated in all the wisdom of the Egyptians? In the Egyptian court, Moses had everything any young man could wish for. He would have had literally hundreds of attendants. Anything Moses wanted was within his reach. Because he was being groomed to be the next ruler of Egypt, he would have been given the very best education in science, military training, and religion. But, he would also have been thoroughly indoctrinated in the Egyptian gods. That can't be good. Some of this training may have been helpful for Moses' later life in leading the Israelites, but how could knowledge of all the false gods of Egypt be helpful? *Fear the Lord and shun evil (Prov 3:7).* At this point, we just have to keep our fingers crossed that the faith of his parents will sustain him. How could all of Moses' education in evil be ordained by God? How could this be part of God's plan? I want you to realize something. All of this is simply God exercising his sovereign control over events and circumstances in order to advance his pre-determined plan. All of Moses' training became useful when dedicated to God. The Apostle Paul was comparable to Moses in that he also received the best training the world had to offer, even though it was error, and yet all of that knowledge was put to use when dedicated to God.

Everything you have learned in life, regardless of the source, becomes useful when placed in God's hand.

Josephus states that Moses became a mighty military leader. Acts 7:22 says that *he was mighty in speech and action*. He was not the humble man the Bible tells us about. In the book of Numbers it states that *Moses was the most humble man on the face of the earth* (Num 12:3). Of course, Moses is the author of Numbers. If Moses was right about himself and he was the most humble man on the face of the earth, then something must have happened in his life after his training in the Egyptian court that served to humble him. I guess we'll have to stay tuned for that.

CHAPTER 5

_____

Moses Accepts God's Destiny for His Life

Now with all of this background, I'd like you to consider one thing. Through his parents, God has given Moses a vision and a destiny for his life. We have seen that Moses was a man with a God-given vision. What made Moses great was that he believed God for the dream he had given him. You and I set off on this journey together to see how we can learn to be men and women of faith like Moses, and to believe God for the vision he has for us. Now as Moses faces a time of crisis and decision in his life, I want us to see how he deals with it and why he makes the decisions he does.

By faith Moses, when he had grown up, refused to be known as the son of Pharaoh's daughter. He chose to be mistreated along with the people of God rather than to enjoy the pleasures of sin for a short time. He regarded disgrace for the sake of Christ as of greater value than the treasures of Egypt, because he was looking ahead to his reward (Heb 11:24-26). Historical sources indicate that when Moses was 20 his foster grandfather, the king, died. Being the son of the rightful heir to the throne, Moses was next in line to be Pharaoh. But Moses refused to take the throne. Being Pharaoh didn't line up with the vision that Jehovah had given him. Imagine that! Moses refused to be promoted to the leader of the most powerful nation on earth because he believed that God had a different dream for his life. Wow! Since Moses refused the throne, Pharaoh's daughter married a half brother who became Pharaoh. But after reigning just a short time, he died. Now 25 years old, Moses was presented with another opportunity to be king. Again, he refused, and the princess married another half brother who became king. This new Pharaoh was a ruthless man and he saw Moses as a threat to his power. When Moses' adoptive mother died, Moses was in great danger. His only protection was that he was still considered royalty. Even with the princess dead, Moses could still call himself her son and afford himself a level of protection, as well as live with all the benefits of royalty. But Read Hebrews 11:24 again: *By faith Moses, when he had grown up, refused to be known as the son of Pharaoh's daughter.* Moses was on a mission to fulfill the dream Jehovah had given him.

God is the giver of dreams and he gives us everything we need to accomplish the dream he gives us.

Think about this. What did Moses have to give up for his dream, and what did he get to keep? He had to give up everything...his future...his life... his safety...his comfort. He gave up being a big shot...being the leader of the most powerful country on the face of the earth. He got to keep his belief that God would provide. Moses gave up everything to gain even more. He took the ultimate risk. He was all in. God was able to give Moses a big dream because he knew that Moses would risk everything for the dream. God wants to give you a big dream too. What are you willing to risk?

When Moses made the choice not to be called the son of Pharaoh's daughter, he disinherited himself from all the riches, pleasures and protection that Egyptian royalty had to offer. He was a man with a dream and a vision. He was to be the Savior and deliverer of his people. Now was his chance to put his Egyptian education and training to good use. Surely a man with Moses' stature and ability was just the right man for God to use to deliver the Israelites. Moses was confident and he was ready for action. Moses was ready to "get busy" doing God's work.

Let's read the story and see what happened: *One day, after Moses had grown up, he went out to where his own people were and watched them at their hard labor. He saw an Egyptian beating a Hebrew, one of his own people. Glancing this way and that and seeing no one, he killed the Egyptian and hid him in the sand. The next day he went out and saw two Hebrews fighting. He asked the one in the wrong, "Why are you hitting your fellow Hebrew?" The man said, "Who made you ruler and judge over us? Are you thinking of killing me as you killed the Egyptian?" Then Moses was afraid and thought, "What I did must have become known." When Pharaoh heard of this, he tried to kill Moses, but Moses fled from Pharaoh and went to live in Midian, where he sat down by a well (Ex 2:11-15).*

Let's look at the same account from Acts: *"When Moses was forty years old, he decided to visit his fellow Israelites. He saw one of them being mistreated by an Egyptian, so he went to his defense and avenged him by killing the Egyptian. Moses thought that his own people would realize that God was using him to rescue them, but they did not. The next day Moses came upon two Israelites who were fighting. He tried to reconcile them by saying, "Men, you are brothers; why do you want to hurt each other?" But the man who was mistreating the other pushed Moses aside and said, "Who made you ruler and judge over us? Do you want to kill me as you killed the Egyptian yesterday?" When Moses heard this, he fled to Midian, where he settled as a foreigner and had two sons (Acts 7:23-29).*

Having disinherited himself from Egypt, Moses tries to identify with his own people. To his surprise, his fellow Israelites do not accept him. I guess, to them he was just another Egyptian. Moses is bewildered and confused - no longer an Egyptian...not yet a Jew. In the crisis, he does just what I would do...he runs. It's called failure!!!!

CHAPTER 6

Failure, the Desert School of Theology

Let's recap a little. Moses is used to living a life of opportunity. He is a man of great power and confidence as the heir to the Egyptian throne. He gives up all of that, but it is in anticipation of leading the Israelites out and being their leader and redeemer. Moses is used to things going his way. He is used to doing things in a big way. He gave up leading a great nation for the prospects of being God's man in leading another great nation.

Moses had given up much to follow God. Where is God now? What a discouragement it must have been now that Moses finds himself basically a man without a country. What might Moses have been tempted to feel or think about Jehovah at this point? Have you ever felt like God gave you something important to do and then when you tried to do it there was no God in sight? What was the problem? Moses was strong for God? Is there such a thing as being too strong for God?

There is a principle at work here. As we began to look at Moses' life, we realized that Moses' story was going to be all about faith. We asked if faith was something we are supposed to have or something God gives us. If we look just a little below the surface here, we will see a principle at work that will help bring some more clarity to that question. God had made his way known to Moses but Moses didn't yet know God's ways. Moses' disappointment with life was in reality an appointment with God. Moses knew what his destiny was, but he had yet to learn to depend on the God who had determined that destiny. Before he could serve God, he had to know God's ways; and so, God enrolled him in what I call "The Desert School of Theology."

In order to have the kind of faith that accomplishes great things for the kingdom of God, we must know God's ways. God enrolls us in the "Desert School of Theology" to teach us his ways; as we submit to his teaching, then faith will rise in us. We look at all the heroes of faith in the Bible and we look for common threads - something that they all shared - so that like them, we can enter into a life of great faith and adventures with Jehovah. This principle is one of the keys we've been looking for. It seems that all of the great faith people of the Bible went to the same school...The Desert School of Theology.

Some examples from scripture of God's Desert School of Theology:

Elijah:

Look at 1Kings 17: *Now Elijah the Tishbite, from Tishbe in Gilead, said to Ahab, "As the LORD, the God of Israel, lives, whom I serve, there will be neither dew nor rain in the next few years except at my word" (verse 1).* In verse 1, Elijah demonstrates that he is bold and committed to the mission that Jehovah has given him. But is he too strong to accomplish what God has given him to do? Look at the following verses: *Then the word of the LORD came to Elijah: "Leave here, turn eastward and hide in the Kerith Ravine, east of the Jordan. You will drink from the brook, and I have ordered the ravens to feed you there." (verse 2)* Kerith is out in the desert. It's a remote desolate place. The word Kerith means "place of failure." God had Elijah in that place of failure for as long as a year. He was teaching Elijah his ways so that Elijah could accomplish what God had for him "by faith." So God was going to instill faith in Elijah at Kerith. Was there anything that Elijah had to do? *So he did what the LORD had told him. He went to the Kerith Ravine, east of the Jordan, and stayed there. The ravens brought him bread and meat in the morning and bread and meat in the evening, and he drank from the brook (verse5, 6).* Elijah had to submit to what God wanted to teach him.

The Apostle Paul:

The Apostle Paul was too strong for God to use. God had given Paul great visions and revelations. He had worked mighty miracles and had even been caught up to the third heaven. He was in danger of being too self-confident and taking himself too seriously: *To keep me from becoming conceited because of these surpassingly great revelations, there was given me a thorn in my flesh, a messenger of Satan, to torment me. Three times I pleaded with the Lord to take it away from me. But he said to me, "My grace is sufficient for you, for my power is made perfect in weakness." Therefore I will boast all the more gladly about my weaknesses, so that Christ's power may rest on me. That is why, for Christ's sake, I delight in weaknesses, in insults, in hardships, in persecutions, in difficulties. For when I am weak, then I am strong (2 Cor 12:7-10).*

Job:

Job was a man with faith in God but God allowed him a desert experience to increase his faith. We all know the story but do you know how Job's story ends? *My ears had heard of you but now my eyes have seen you (Job 42:5).*

The desert school is hard, but graduating from it always results in a clearer view of God.

Knowing this should help us embrace the times of failure in our lives.

On and on it goes. The Bible gives us example after example. Jonah's schooling was in the belly of a whale. Naomi's desert came when her husband died. Read the Psalms and you quickly realize that God brought David back to the desert school over and over. Has God ever enrolled you in the Desert School of Theology? Think about times in your life when your whole world seemed to come crashing down around you. How did you respond? What was the result? As we will see, there was a dramatic difference in Moses' life after the Desert.

Stop just for a moment and consider something. We all know that in our own strength we don't accomplish much for the Kingdom of God, and we know that God isn't impressed with our fleshly efforts. We all know that in our own strength nothing much happens, but that there is no limit to what we can do if we have God's strength at our disposal, right? What I'd like you to consider is this. God is not in the business of giving us his strength so that we can accomplish great things. What God really wants is that we would simply surrender ourselves to him. *Therefore, I urge you, brothers, in view of God's mercy, to offer your bodies as living sacrifices, holy and pleasing to God--this is your spiritual act of worship (Rom 12:1).* Now a sacrifice is generally dead. In the Old Testament, a lamb would be killed and then sacrificed to the Lord. But God wants us to be living sacrifices. He doesn't give us strength to do great things; we give him our lives, and he lives in us to do great things. So it's no longer me who lives but Christ lives in me.

CHAPTER 7

_____

The Backside of the Desert

Now the Bible doesn't tell us much about Moses' life during the 40 years that God schooled him in the desert. Elijah spent as much as a year alone with God at Kerith, but we aren't given any details. Maybe the Holy Sprit has purposefully left out the details of when he was alone with his intimates; he knows that each of our experiences with him will be unique. We can, however, tell much about Moses' time in the desert by taking a before and after snapshot.

Before the desert Moses was a brash, confident and bold warrior. He was sold out to God but he wasn't dead to self. *When Pharaoh heard of this, he tried to kill Moses, but Moses fled from Pharaoh and went to live in Midian, where he sat down by a well. Now a priest of Midian had seven daughters, and they came to draw water and fill the troughs to water their father's flock. Some shepherds came along and drove them away, but Moses got up and came to their rescue and watered their flock (Ex 2:15-17).* Moses rescued the Jewish slave from the Egyptian but that got him into a lot of trouble. Now he is rescuing the fair maidens at the well. Before his time at the desert school, Moses had the heart of a rescuer but wasn't surrendered to the will of the Lord. Let's take a peek at Moses after the desert and see if we notice a difference. *"So now, go (Moses). I am sending you to Pharaoh to bring my people the Israelites out of Egypt."* But Moses said to God, *"Who am I that I should go to Pharaoh and bring the Israelites out of Egypt?" (Ex 3:10-11).* Before the desert, Moses could rescue seven girls from some bully shepherds at the well. After the desert, God was able to use Moses to bring four million people out from bondage. Don't fight God or get angry with God when life finds you in the desert. Learn the lesson from every great man and woman in the Bible. Use your time in the desert to allow God to care for and comfort you there. When you fail, God isn't punishing or ignoring you; he is preparing you for better things. Learn to lean on him.

CHAPTER 8

Graduation day at the Bush

Now Moses was tending the flock of Jethro his father-in-law, the priest of Midian, and he led the flock to the far side of the desert and came to Horeb, the mountain of God. There the angel of the LORD appeared to him in flames of fire from within a bush. Moses saw that though the bush was on fire it did not burn up. So Moses thought, "I will go over and see this strange sight--why the bush does not burn up." When the LORD saw that he had gone over to look, God called to him from within the bush,

"Moses! Moses!" And Moses said, "Here I am" *(Exodus 3:1-4).*

Moses has spent 40 years in the desert school of life. Like all schools, there comes a time of graduation. Moses had spent 40 years under God's tutelage. He was ready now for God to use to deliver his people. God had promised the Jews that after 400 years he would redeem them. God had told Abraham: *Know for certain that your descendants will be strangers in a country not their own, and they will be enslaved and mistreated four hundred years. But I will punish the nation they serve as slaves, and afterward they will come out with great possessions (Genesis 15:13-14).* The 400 years were now up. God was preparing to make good on his promise. The burning bush became Moses' commissioning service. Jehovah was about to give the commencement address. And yet even though he was graduating, Moses still had several important lessons to learn. That day was to become the turning point in his life. After the burning bush Moses was never the same again.

God called Moses' name twice. From that moment on, Moses' entire life would be different. The call of God would completely change any plans that Moses had for his future. From this time on it was God's agenda. In the desert, Moses had learned his lessons well. His Egyptian education had taught Moses to be a man of action. The Bible says that in Egypt Moses was a man of great deeds and words. He was the leader of the greatest army in the world and he had fought and won many battles. But God's school of the desert had changed Moses. He no longer had an emphasis on deeds but saw the need of being in right relationship with God – of being what God wanted him to be. His life only existed now as it existed "in God." The school of the desert, the place of helplessness and failure, teaches us to be quiet. Some of us will learn that "being" is more important than "doing" through tragedy or pain or failure. If that is true in your life, then you are in good company. God put Moses in the desert place of failure for 40 years so he could become possibly the most well-known leader the world has ever known - but it would no longer be through trying, but through trusting.

Why a burning bush? The burning bush incident was about to become Moses' life-changing encounter with God. Knowledge by hearsay was about to become knowledge by experience. Remember the same thing happened to Job. *My ears had heard of you but now my eyes have seen you (Job 42:5).* Moses' own self-confidence had led him from the next great leader of the most powerful country on earth to a nobody. The burning bush transformed Moses from an unknown desert shepherd to possibly the greatest leader the world has ever known. Think about it. God called Moses to lead upwards to four million people out into the desert where their only hope for survival was if God himself would take care of them. There was nothing to eat or drink in the desert. There was nowhere to find shelter from the blistering sun by day or the freezing cold by night. There was no way to get new clothes when theirs wore out; no way to live except as Jehovah provided. His many years in the desert had prepared Moses for this moment. God knew this, but Moses did not.

The burning bush gives us some beautiful symbolism. This isn't the only time where God appeared as fire. In the Bible, "fire" symbolizes the glory of the Lord. *To the Israelites, the glory of the LORD looked like a consuming fire on top of the mountain (Ex 24:17).* Okay, I understand fire. I would expect God to show up in something like fire, but why a bush? Why not have a huge tree on fire, or an entire mountain. God is a big God. Surely he could have put on a really big show. Why just an ordinary bush? If you can picture a tumble weed before it breaks off and goes blowing across the desert, you have a pretty good picture of the bush. If you were walking in the desert and you came across this burning bush would you say, "Oh look, an ordinary bush"? No, of course not; you would say, "Look!! Fire!!" The bush was ordinary but it was the fire, the presence of God that made it extraordinary. The burning bush was perfect for Moses' graduation because it symbolized what he had become. Egypt had taught Moses men's idea of greatness. The Desert School of Theology had taught him true greatness. Moses had learned that the important thing about his life was not himself but the glory of God revealed through him. What a lesson for you and me.

True greatness is when someone looks at you and sees Jesus!

True greatness is when you are so ordinary that when others see you they only see the presence of the living God burning in your life. That fire of God that changed Moses forever is the same fire that God wants for you. Think about those tongues of fire that appeared above the disciples of Jesus in that upper room after Jesus' crucifixion. Before Pentecost, the disciples fled from their enemies. But at Pentecost, they were given a holy boldness that changed their lives forever. Jesus had promised them the presence of God as manifested by the Holy Spirit: *But you will receive power when the Holy Spirit comes on you; and you will be my witnesses in Jerusalem, and in all*

Judea and Samaria, and to the ends of the earth" (Acts 1:8). In that upper room they were praying for the Holy Sprit as Jesus had promised. Look at what happened: *When the day of Pentecost came, they were all together in one place. Suddenly a sound like the blowing of a violent wind came from heaven and filled the whole house where they were sitting. They saw what seemed to be tongues of fire that separated and came to rest on each of them. All of them were filled with the Holy Spirit and began to speak in other tongues as the Spirit enabled them* (Acts 2:1-4). Wow! Fire came to be the symbol of God's empowering presence.

If you haven't received God's commissioning call on your life, pray and ask him for it. But then you must be willing to attend the Desert School of Theology where He will teach you how to be an ordinary bush. When you have learned the lesson of humility, you will be set on fire with the power to transform lives with your testimony.

CHAPTER 9

God's Commissioning Call

When the LORD saw that he had gone over to look, God called to him from within the bush, "Moses! Moses!" And Moses said, "Here I am." "Do not come any closer," God said. "Take off your sandals, for the place where you are standing is holy ground." Then he said, "I am the God of your father, the God of Abraham, the God of Isaac and the God of Jacob." At this, Moses hid his face, because he was afraid to look at God (Ex 3:4-6).

Let's look at some more of the symbolism with what is happening here. Look at these verses and notice two things that Moses did. At Jehovah's direction

Moses took his shoes off and then Moses hid his face. First shoes - shoes remind me of doing. When I got saved, one of the first things I learned was, "You need to put shoe leather to your theology." The idea was that I shouldn't be complacent about my Christian service; to be a good Christian I should get busy. Since then I've come to understand a higher truth. If someone needs to tell me to put shoe leather to my theology, then my theology is flawed and my picture of who God is and what he has done for me is defective. If someone needs to tell me to get busy, then that is the last thing I should do.

A bush doesn't get busy to be great; it develops a relationship with the fire.

I think the church struggles with this concept. I think sometimes we communicate a subtle message that doing equals holiness. In the church we are often led to believe that success lies in well-attended programs. Individuals are given the subtle message that regular attendance and supporting the different programs of the church is what makes for a good Christian. Sometimes the message isn't so subtle. The all importance of the empowering presence of the Holy Spirit in our lives can be washed away in a flurry of activity. As a church we need to guard ourselves from this, and as individuals we need to realize that it's okay to just be an ordinary bush. It's not what we can do that is important, but what Jesus can do in us.

Next, Moses hid his face. This reminds me of humility. My human nature wants to be recognized. I want people to see me and like me. Too often I am guilty of working for the praise of men.

Moses was commanded to take off his shoes because God was not interested in his human activity. *Take off your shoes Moses* because you are in the presence of God. Moses hid his face because he was aware of his own unworthiness before God...two lessons learned on the backside of the desert.

When the LORD saw that he had gone over to look, God called to him from within the bush, "Moses! Moses!" (Ex 3:4). God called out Moses' name twice and stopped him in his tracks. Are you ready for your own commissioning, your own burning bush experience? Only those whose hearts are quiet enough to hear his voice are ready. A recurring phrase that you'll see in the Bible is *"Let him who has an ear, hear."* God wants to speak to you by his spirit and through his word. Are you quiet enough to hear his voice? In the quietness of his heart Moses learned that what he could not do by force God would accomplish by faith. When God spoke, Moses' instant reaction was, "Here I am Lord." Are you ready to hear the voice of God? When you are ready to receive, then God will set you on fire and you will begin to draw others to him.

The LORD said, "I have indeed seen the misery of my people in Egypt. I have heard them crying out because of their slave drivers, and I am concerned about their suffering. So I have come down to rescue them from the hand of the Egyptians and to bring them up out of that land into a good and spacious land, a land flowing with milk and honey...And now the cry of the Israelites has reached me, and I have seen the way the Egyptians are oppressing them. So now, go. I am sending you to Pharaoh to bring my people the Israelites out of Egypt" (Ex 3:7-10). "I have seen the misery of my people. I have heard them crying. I have come down to rescue them." Maybe Moses is finally getting the idea that he is not the one who is going to be the savior of Israel. Maybe he is beginning to realize that all of God's work must begin with God. He has spent many years striving and finally mourning over his own failure. Now he begins to see that the plan must first originate with Jehovah.

But then he hears these words: *"So now, go. I am sending you to Pharaoh to bring my people the Israelites out of Egypt."* Moses responds, "Whoa God, don't say that now. I've been there, done that, and with not such good results." Of course, what God was saying was that he was going to save Israel from the Egyptians and that he was going to use Moses.

With this discourse, Moses was at the third great faith crisis of his life. The first was at his birth, which was really a crisis of faith for his parents. The second was when Moses by faith refused to be called the son of Pharaoh's daughter. This third crisis is also a crisis of faith. Moses is being called by God to go back to the place where he failed and do the thing he failed to do. He is being asked to deliver the very people who rejected him as their deliverer. How do you think Moses felt hearing these words from God? Why are things different now? He failed before. Why might he succeed now? Before, it was Moses' plan to deliver the Israelites. He may have even prayed and asked God to help him do it, but it was his thing. This time, it is God who has decided to deliver Israel and he is asking Moses to be his instrument.

In Stephen's account of the burning bush, he says that Moses trembled at the voice of God. *"I am the*

God of your fathers, the God of Abraham, Isaac and Jacob." Moses trembled with fear and did not dare to look (Acts 7:32). The Apostle John heard the voice of the Lord on the Island of Patmos and he trembled. Saul of Tarsus heard the voice of the Lord on the way to Damascus to persecute the Christians. It knocked him off his horse. Does God still speak today? How do you hear the voice of God? *In the past, God spoke to our forefathers through the prophets at many times and in various ways, but in these last days he has spoken to us by his Son, whom he appointed heir of all things, and through whom he made the universe (Heb 1:1-2).*

Moses and the Israelites never forgot this "burning bush" where Moses heard God speak. The place became known as the "Mountain of God." Make sure that there is a place where you can hear the voice of God. There is no greater need in our Christian lives. To have a relationship with Jesus we must hear his voice. God is not hiding. He created you to have a relationship with him. The Bible says that if we seek him we will find him. He has given us the Bible and his Spirit that we might connect with him. If we will seek him in the pages of his book, and if we will listen for his Spirit, we will hear him.

At the burning bush, Moses heard God's commissioning call on his life. God has given us a similar calling in the New Testament: *You did not choose me, but I chose you and appointed you to go and bear fruit--fruit that will last. Then the Father will give you whatever you ask in my name (John 15:16).*

CHAPTER 10

The Conquest of Inferiority

God chose Moses and he is molding him into the person he created him to be. In the forty years in the desert God has dealt with the self-reliance Moses learned in the Egyptian court. Now the burning bush becomes for Moses the conquest of inferiority. *But Moses said to God, "Who am I that I should go to Pharaoh and bring the Israelites out of Egypt?" (Ex 3:11).* Can you relate to Moses here? Moses still doesn't quite get it...as though he had to be somebody. Inferiority always comes back to the place of "who am I"? The root of inferiority is pride just as with self-reliance. Pride is when it's all about you, whether you think too highly of yourself or think of yourself as nothing. Don't you love God's answer: *And God said, "I will be with you... (Ex 3:12).* Don't slide over this verse too quickly if you have struggled with self-image or inferiority.

God's five-word cure for an inferiority complex - "I will be with you."

Moses failed last time. How can he be sure that same failure won't repeat itself this time? God tells him that he won't fail this time because - *"it is I who has sent you."* The truth is, when we are in the center of God's will we cannot fail. *Moses said to God, "Suppose I go to the Israelites and say to them, 'The God of your fathers has sent me to you,' and they ask me, 'What is his name?' Then what shall I tell them?" (Ex 3:13).* Moses isn't quite convinced. His past failures have taught him to fear men; his fear runs deep. He still remembers his rejection in Egypt by the Israelites. Those words still ring in his ears - *"Who has given you the right to judge between us?"* It was a question that he couldn't answer. Now he anticipates finding himself in that same position. He realizes that he has no authority in Egypt. This prompts the question about God's name so he can tell them who has sent him. *God said to Moses, "I AM WHO I AM. This is what you are to say to the Israelites: 'I AM has sent me to you'" (Ex 3:14).*

I think this verse is so significant and so applicable to us today. The words, "I am" literally mean: "The God who exists." God was telling Moses to tell the Israelites, "I am the God who is. I am not the God that 400 years in idolatrous Egypt has taught you. I am not the God of your imagination or your expectation. I am the God who is. I am not the God you've heard about or the impotent God the Egyptians think I am. I AM WHO I AM!" Why is this important for us today? It's important because we all have a certain perception of who God is. Maybe our parents taught us about God. Maybe we've been in churches and we've heard what God is like. We've all grown up in Egypt where the world has indoctrinated us with its false sense of who God is. We need to let go of the God of our perceptions and seek the God who is.

I met a young woman a while ago that was in a group I was teaching. She had been abused by her church and her husband. The church publicly chastised her for wearing pants and for putting on makeup. They called her an immoral woman and encouraged her husband to beat her until she submitted. Eventually, she left her husband and the church. She came to this group I was teaching and after a couple of weeks she spoke up. She said, "How can you talk about this God of yours like he is some kind of a merciful God? I don't want to have anything to do with God!" I told her that my God is not the God she thinks he is. He is not the God of her husband. He is not the God her church taught her about. I challenged her to let go of the God she has heard about and discover the God who is. When we get serious about knowing him, when we search for him with all our hearts, and when we pour over his love letter to us and the Holy Spirit begins to open the eyes of our hearts, then we begin to see I AM, the God who is.

So God tells Moses that he is going to use him to deliver Israel and Moses' first response is, "I can't do it." God says, "Moses, read my lips, I didn't ask you to do it." I AM is going to deliver Israel. We have to come to the place where we see that when it comes to God, we are not independent persons; we are his creation, his possession, his instrument.

Imagine for a moment that you have a fishing pole (that can talk). You say to the fishing pole, "I'm going to use you to catch fish." The fishing pole responds with, "No, not me! I can't catch fish. I don't have hands. I can't bait my hook. I can't cast my line into the water. I don't have eyes. I don't even know where the water is. I can't reel in. Sorry, I just can't do it." You say to the fishing pole: "But I will be with you. It's all together different when I am with you. All of your inabilities vanish as you become merely an instrument in my hands. I am the one who is fishing and I am using you." And so God says to you, "I am going to use you to fish for men." "Oh, no," you say. "I'm not an evangelist, I'm not good with words, and I can't do it." God says, "But I will be with you." You see the skill of the instrument is of little value but what is vitally important is that the instrument be intimately connected and available to the master. Our own strength and talent is of no importance, but what is important is that we be invested with the presence and the power of God.

In order to be used of God, we need to be emptied of self and filled with God. Forty years in the desert had emptied Moses of self. The burning bush was the occasion of being filled with God. Moses was a different man after the burning bush. The burning bush was a picture of the man Moses was to become; a common, ordinary man, aflame with the fire of God. In Egypt, Moses came to believe that he was special, that he was born for a purpose, and that he was extraordinary. In the desert, Moses became common and ordinary. On the mountain of God as he faced the burning bush, Moses learned that the significance didn't lie in him at all, but in whether or not he was invested with the presence and the power of God.

And so fellow bushes...are you ready to catch fire?
Do you think God's promise to Moses will carry over
to us today? *Then Jesus came to them and said, "All
authority in heaven and on earth has been given to
me. Therefore go and make disciples of all nations,
baptizing them in the name of the Father and of the
Son and of the Holy Spirit, and teaching them to obey
everything I have commanded you. And surely I am
with you always, to the very end of the age"* (Matt
28:18-20).

CHAPTER 11

This Time it's God's Way

And so, at Moses' commissioning service at the burning bush, Jehovah lays out his plan for Moses. *Go, assemble the elders of Israel and say to them, "The LORD, the God of your fathers--the God of Abraham, Isaac and Jacob--appeared to me and said: 'I have watched over you and have seen what has been done to you in Egypt. And I have promised to bring you up out of your misery in Egypt into the land of the Canaanites, Hittites, Amorites, Perizzites, Hivites and Jebusites--a land flowing with milk and honey. The elders of Israel will listen to you. Then you and the elders are to go to the king of Egypt and say to him, 'The LORD, the God of the Hebrews, has met with us. Let us take a three-day journey into the desert to offer sacrifices to the LORD our God.' But I know that the king of Egypt will not let you go unless a mighty hand compels him. So I will stretch out my hand and strike the Egyptians with all the wonders that I will perform among them. After that, he will let you go. "And I will make the Egyptians favorably disposed toward this people, so that when you leave you will not go empty-handed. Every woman is to ask her neighbor and any woman living in her house for articles of silver and gold and for clothing, which you will put on your sons and daughters. And so you will plunder the Egyptians" (Ex3:16-22).*

When God gives you a dream, he will also at some point give you a plan for accomplishing the dream? The Bible shows us a pattern of how God deals with us. First, he gives us a dream, then he prepares us, and then he gives us marching orders. Many times we get this sequence confused in our lives. Sometimes we go off without God at all and seek after our own dreams. Sometimes we receive a dream from God but run ahead without first being prepared. Remember that when God gives you a dream it is he who will bring it about. We only need to submit ourselves to his process.

I think about how he led many of the Bible characters with specific instructions:

Elijah...Jehoshaphat...Gideon. Then I think of Joseph who God seemed to take from one calamity to another without any specific instructions. What I get from this is that we can't lock God into any particular formula for how he will prepare and guide us in the thing he has for us to do. He may not even reveal the whole vision to us. What is important is that we are ready to take the next step as he reveals it and that we trust him. Always know that he is with you and he is for you.

Next we have Moses' reaction to God's plan: *Moses answered, "What if they do not believe me or listen to me and say, 'The LORD did not appear to you?'" (Ex 4:1).* What do you think of Moses' reaction, legitimate or not? What had God already told Moses in Ex 3:18:*"The elders of Israel will listen to you."* How often do we fail to hear God's voice because it contradicts our own reasoning? Part of letting go of our own agenda and being open to what God has for us involves letting go of our human reasoning in the face of God's command to go. Now put yourself in the place of the Israelites. Does Moses have any reason to believe that the Israelites will listen to him when he comes back and tells them about how God has now decided to rescue them? What credentials does Moses bring? In Egypt, he had his titles and his degrees and his honors. He was part of the royal family. He had every reason to believe that when he went to the Israelites they would accept him as their leader, and yet they didn't. They rejected him. Now

---

after 40 years in the desert as a shepherd is there any reason for him to think that they'll listen now? Moses felt he lacked for the task ahead. It should have been enough that God told Moses they would listen, but it wasn't enough. Moses was just like you and me. In any case, Moses' concern over authority didn't go unanswered. It was important that the Israelites looked up to Moses and had confidence in him. *Then the LORD said to him, "What is that in your hand?" "A staff," he replied. The LORD said, "Throw it on the ground" (Ex 4:2-3).* There is so much for us in these two verses. What did Moses have in his hand? It was a shepherd's rod. In Egypt, shepherds were the most despised of all people, and the staff would not be an appropriate symbol of Moses' authority. A golden scepter would be better. Even though the rod was a foolish symbol of authority to the Egyptians, it was to have a great future in the events of Moses' life. Why didn't God provide an appropriate "golden scepter" for Moses? Why a lowly shepherd's rod? Maybe this rod uncovers an important principle of how God operates.

It seems that God often chooses the weakest instruments in order to accomplish the mightiest deeds.

80

The Lord told Joshua to march around Jericho seven times and then blow rams horns to defeat Jericho. I can hear Joshua saying, "Lord, how are we going to defeat Jericho...the walls are so high." God responds with, "What do you have in your hand Joshua?" Sampson killed a thousand Philistines with the jawbone of a donkey. Gideon and his 300 men attacked 100,000 Midianites with clay pitchers. When David took Goliath on, I can picture him crying out to God and asking him how he could defeat this giant. I picture God asking David, "What do you have in your hand?" David looks down at a simple sling.

What do you have in your hand?

What do you have to fight your battles and defeat the enemies in your life? What do you have that equips you to be the person God made you to be and do the things that he has for you to do? Is what you have in your hand enough? Was the sling enough for David? Were the clay pots enough for Gideon? Was the jawbone enough for Sampson? Was the shepherd's rod enough for Moses? The principle is that when anything is used by God, no matter how insignificant, it can perform the task he assigns it. So, a rod with Jehovah behind it is more powerful than all the armies of Pharaoh. Why do you think God chose a shepherd's staff? As God used him in a mighty way, Moses would never be tempted to think that what was being accomplished was because of his own training or ability. In Moses' hand it was just a shepherd's staff. But it became the rod of God, a symbol of omnipotence.

How would you like to have Moses' staff? Would it be easier for you to navigate life if you had the authority of God at your very fingertips? Listen to this! You have all that Moses had and more. The rod became to Moses what Jesus is to us today. Despised by the world, Jesus is the symbol of our authority. The Bible says that all authority has been given to Jesus and Jesus gives that authority to us as we go about the work he has given us to do. In the staff, Moses found all the power and authority he needed to accomplish God's will for his life. In Jesus, we find everything we need.

Moses had his burning bush where God revealed himself to him. We have Eph 1:18: *I pray also that the eyes of your heart may be enlightened in order that you may know the hope to which he has called you, the riches of his glorious inheritance in the saints...* Moses had his rod. We have: *...his incomparably great power for us who believe. That power is like the working of his mighty strength, which he exerted in Christ when he raised him from* *the dead and seated him at his right hand in the heavenly realms, far above all rule and authority, power and dominion, and every title that can be given, not only in the present age but also in the one to come. And God placed all things under his feet and appointed him to be head over everything for the church, which is his body, the fullness of him who fills everything in every way (Eph 1:19-23). "...His incomparably great power is for us!!"* Wow! Think of it. You are God's greatest achievement. He made you on his very best day. You are to be on display forever as his best work. You are a living work of God, not on display as some statue or sculpture. Just like Moses, God has great and mighty works for each one of us and he has made his incomparably great power available to us to accomplish the work he has given us to do. *For we are God's workmanship (poem), created in Christ Jesus to do good works, which God prepared in advance for us to do (Eph 2:10).* We are a living work, created to do great and mighty things in the name of our God. Are you up to it? Can you do great things in the name of your God? God has given you (past tense) his incomparably great power.

God makes HIS power available to us to live as his masterpiece creation. Knowing that, do you think you can get through the week? Do you think you can hang on this week? Will you make it? Does that sound right to you?...that you have the power of God at your disposal and you're wondering if you can hang on and somehow get through the week? Paul here prays that us believers would "know" or "experience" this power. He knew that we would never be able to use the power of God to do great things for God if we didn't believe we had it; so he prays that God would open our eyes.

Pause and pray this prayer with me. "We believe you Jesus. We believe that you have created us and that you have pre-destined us to be your prized possession for all eternity. We believe that our lives are to be on display as your very best achievement on your very best creative day. We believe that we are the only creatures in all your creation capable of containing and passing on your love. Jesus, we believe that we are important to you, that we are valuable, that we are meant to do great and mighty deeds in the name of our God. We pray that as we each take the thing that is in our hand and consecrate it to you, that for us it will become the rod of God just as the staff did for Moses. Jesus, we want you to be the rod of God in our lives. We want all authority and power to be in you as we bring your love to a lost and dying people enslaved in their own Egypt."

CHAPTER 12

_____

Jehovah Equips Moses for the Task He Has Given Him

Then the LORD said to him, "What is that in your hand?" "A staff," he replied. The LORD said, "Throw it on the ground" (Ex 4:2-3). Moses' staff reminds me of my hiking stick. When I'm in the woods my hiking stick is important to me. It is an extension of my arm and it is a third leg. It's useful for balance and a lot of other things, and gives me a sense of security. I don't expect you to understand this unless you are a backpacker, but this stick makes me feel stronger and helps me hike longer. I think Moses' staff was very important to him.

And so Moses is standing in front of the burning bush and he is having this conversation with Jehovah. God has told him that he will be going back to Egypt and that he will be leading his people out. Moses certainly doesn't feel up to the task. He doesn't feel like he is equipped to face either Pharaoh or the Israelites. And now God says, "What's in your hand, Moses?" Moses looks at the staff, one of the few things in his life that he derives a sense of security from. And God says, "Throw it down, Moses." I can imagine Moses' reply, "But God, you don't understand. This staff is important to me." "THROW IT DOWN MOSES!" "But Lord, I use it to herd the sheep, keep my balance, fight off enemies, and to..." "THROW IT DOWN MOSES!" "But Lord I..." "THROW IT DOWN MOSES!"

It may seem like a small thing to us, but the one thing that Moses had that made him feel self-assured was the one thing that God asked him to throw down. Moses had to throw down the one thing he had left that made him feel strong. He had to take the last of his self-assurance and literally throw it at God's feet. For a moment think about the things in your life that give you confidence. Is it the way you look or some talent or spiritual gift? Think about what you are really good at. What are you known for? What in your life makes you feel strong?

Whatever it is in your life that helps you be self-assured, God wants you to throw it down. Why do you think God would want you to let go of something good?

The LORD said, "Throw it on the ground." Moses threw it on the ground and it became a snake, and he ran from it (Ex 4:3). So Moses threw his staff on the ground and it became a snake. Now Moses was no stranger to snakes. He had been living in the desert for 40 years. He was living in prime snake country. Why do you think he ran? Maybe he was just surprised. Or maybe the snake meant something to Moses. The snake was worshipped by the Egyptians and represented the power of Egypt. Maybe when Moses saw the snake he was reminded of the power of Egypt and Pharaoh and ran from that. As he ran, maybe he was crying, "Lord, don't make me go back there!!"

Then the LORD said to him, "Reach out your hand and take it by the tail." So Moses reached out and took hold of the snake and it turned back into a staff in his hand. "This," said the LORD, "is so that they may believe that the LORD, the God of their fathers-- the God of Abraham, the God of Isaac and the God of Jacob--has appeared to you" (Ex 4:4-5). "Reach out my hand and take it by the tail!" – Come on Lord...I

87

didn't just get off the turnip truck! Everyone knows you don't pick up a snake by the tail. Even those who have never picked up a snake know intuitively that you don't pick it up by the tail. Why did God specifically tell Moses to pick up the snake by the tail? He could have just told him to pick it up. Why by the tail? You would never pick up a snake by the tail unless you knew for certain that the snake couldn't hurt you. That was precisely God's point. He was telling Moses that he could trust him and that he would protect him from Pharaoh. The important part of this little exchange between Moses and Jehovah was that God had asked Moses to trust him by picking up the snake by the tail. If I were Moses I would be tempted to argue just a little bit here with God. "Look LORD, I've been living out here in this desert for 40 years now and I know all about snakes. If I pick it up by the tail it will turn on me and bite me and that snake is poisonous." That's what I might have said, but the scripture tells us that Moses simply reached over and picked it up by the tail. Almost every little scene in this "Moses story" brings us back to faith. God is a God who wants to be believed and trusted and if we will trust him he will use each one of us in mighty ways. We have to trust him because his thoughts are not our thoughts (Is

55:8). We can trust him because he is always loving and faithful (Ps 25:10).

God wants us to love him, and more than anything, he wants us to trust him. If you follow God, he will often put you in a place where you must trust him. He will continually test your trust. You may lose your job and he will ask you to trust him. The Lord may give you assignments that are way beyond your own abilities because he wants you to trust him to come through. He may even ask you to pick up a snake by the tail.

Then the Lord said to him, "Reach out your hand and take it by the tail." So Moses reached out and took hold of the snake and it turned back into a staff in his hand (Ex 4:4). Let's not miss the symbolism here. Moses throws his staff on the ground and gives up the thing that has brought him a sense of security in the desert. It becomes a snake representing all the power and might of Egypt, and Moses runs from it. But then, at God's direction, Moses reaches out and takes hold of the snake in such a way as to be completely vulnerable and unable to protect himself. He places himself totally in God's hands. God then turns the snake back into a staff, giving back to Moses the thing that was so meaningful and important to him. But now it is no longer Moses' staff. Now, it is the "Rod of God." Moses has his staff back, but he no longer derives his sense of security and protection from it. Now God is the source of his strength. The Holy Spirit has given us this picture because God wants to do the same thing in our lives. He wants us to throw at his feet everything in our lives that gives us a sense of accomplishment; he wants us to throw down everything that gives us a sense of security. He wants us to give him all our "things" so that he can consecrate them and give them back to us.

I can imagine in Egypt someone asking Moses, "Where did you get that staff?" Before the burning bush he might have answered, "I fashioned it myself from a piece of wood." But now Moses simply answers..."It's not my staff, it belongs to Jehovah. He gave it to me." Jesus wants all of our possessions and abilities to be consecrated to him in this way.

God demonstrated to Moses that he (Jehovah) had authority over the serpent. God would crush the power of Egypt now, and in the future, Satan himself would be defeated at the cross. *Since the children have flesh and blood, he too shared in their humanity so that by his death he might destroy him who holds the power of death--that is, the devil (Heb 2:14).*

Moses is now equipped with the "Rod of God", but Jehovah continues to give him what he needs to face Pharaoh. *Then the LORD said, "Put your hand inside your cloak." So Moses put his hand into his cloak, and when he took it out, it was leprous, like snow. "Now put it back into your cloak," he said. So Moses put his hand back into his cloak, and when he took it out, it was restored, like the rest of his flesh (Ex 4:6-7).* God gave Moses these signs to convince Egypt, yet he knew they wouldn't move Pharaoh. Why these signs? In the Bible, leprosy is symbolic of sin. Moses puts his hand to his heart and it comes out dirty; it represents who Moses is. His hand represents his actions, and his actions are sinful because they come from a sinful heart. Then Moses puts his hand to his heart again and it comes out healthy. This represents who Moses is to become. God wanted not only the staff but Moses himself consecrated, so he could cleanse his heart. Moses would need a pure heart so his hand would be pure and fit to hold the "Rod of God." Again, the symbolism shouldn't escape us. Remember, we have a God who loves to use our lives to paint pictures. Just as God took the leprosy from Moses' hand, so the son of man takes away the sin in our lives.

CHAPTER 13

God is All We Need

Moses has been standing at the burning bush for a while now. I am slow to lead us on from here because I believe that the next level of our Christian life begins here at the bush. Many of us lead lives similar to Moses' on the backside of the desert. He spent his time mostly just trying to get through the days. He would wake up every morning to the same life. He would spend his days trying to keep the sand out of his shoes, taking care of the sheep, eating, sleeping and hoping for a better day tomorrow. If you could go back to those days and ask Moses how his life is going, he might say something like – "Life is okay. The sheep are fed. I hope there won't be a sand storm today. I hope those wolves keep their distance. Oy vey! The stories I could tell you about those wolves!" Most of Moses' time was spent dealing with the nits of life, and I think that is where many of us dwell. Many of us dwell in the land of making it through until Friday. That's the way Moses' life was, but all that changed at the burning bush.

Put yourself in Moses' place as we continue his discourse with Jehovah. *Moses said to the LORD, "O Lord, I have never been eloquent, neither in the past nor since you have spoken to your servant. I am slow of speech and tongue" (Ex 4:10).* Moses is not convinced that he is the man the Lord should send to Egypt. He has failed before, and he is afraid he may fail again. The Lord has put a love for Israel in his heart and he has called him to go, but Moses is afraid of failure - he raises one objection after another arguing why he shouldn't go. Moses doubted that he was man enough for the job, but God wasn't looking for a man with sufficient abilities. He was just looking for a man who would believe.

Do you want to have great adventures with God? Ask yourself that question right now. In your heart right now, ask yourself if you want a dream for a great adventure with God. My guess is that confronted with this question most people would say, "Yes."

Who wouldn't want to be mightily used by God? The problem is that as soon as we say yes to that question, then doubts about our ability start to rise. We limit the size of the dream that God can give us to our own feeble abilities. The good news is that God doesn't need any abilities on your part to give you a great dream. The ability lies in him. God isn't looking for people who are mighty in deeds. He is simply looking for people who will stand. The truth is expressed in Ezekiel 22:30: *I looked for a man among them who would build up the wall and stand before me in the gap on behalf of the land so I would not have to destroy it, but I found none.*

While men and women seek methods, God merely seeks men and women who are available.

We people are too prone to put our trust in methods or organizations and institutions to accomplish our goals. We tend to think that the big ideas have to come from the church leaders or the pastor. Often the pastor or leaders plan the ministry and then they try to motivate the people to get on board. If you have been in a church for a while, then you've probably received numerous calls and e-mails letting you know how badly you are needed to help with this program or that. To the church's shame, we often even result in guilt motivation because it works. But God is different. He works with individuals, not institutions. He wants people surrendered to him, people he can bless by accomplishing his dream in them. God is simply looking for people who will stand. He will fill us with the abilities we need so that he can accomplish his goals through us.

If you are willing, don't you think God will give you a dream that is way beyond your own abilities? *For the eyes of the Lord range throughout the earth to strengthen those whose hearts are fully committed to him...(2 Chronicles 16:9).* This verse says that God is actively seeking those who will join him in his adventures. Wow!! Look at that verse carefully. It does not say that the Lord will strengthen you. It says that he will show himself strong. What is the difference? You see, in the great adventure that Jesus will give you, God is not going to strengthen you for the task; instead, he is going to show himself strong on your behalf.

Listen to the Lord's response to Moses' next objection, because it is an important lesson for us: *The LORD said to him, "Who gave man his mouth? Who makes him deaf or mute? Who gives him sight or makes him blind? Is it not I, the LORD? Now go; I will help you speak and will teach you what to say"*

(Ex 4:11-12). This verse reminds me of 2 Cor 12:9: *But he said to me, "My grace is sufficient for you, for my power is made perfect in weakness." Therefore I will boast all the more gladly about my weaknesses, so that Christ's power may rest on me (2 Corinthians 12:9).*

Like Paul, and eventually Moses, we also need to realize that God's grace is sufficient for us as well. What Moses had to learn at the burning bush was that with God he was invincible. What we need to learn is that in Christ we are invincible. *It is because of him that you are in Christ Jesus, who has become for us wisdom from God--that is, our righteousness, holiness and redemption. Therefore, as it is written: "Let him who boasts boast in the Lord" (1 Cor 1:30-31).* This verse gives us a very good picture of what it means to be "in Christ." When God gives you a dream, then he equips you for the task. If you need wisdom, then he becomes wisdom for you. If you need righteousness, then Jesus is your righteousness. If you need holiness and redemption, then it is his holiness and redemption that you can lean on. You see, Jesus is all we need. The only thing that must happen for us to have great adventures with God is our eyes need to be opened so we can see that he is all we need. *I pray also that the eyes of your heart may be enlightened in order that you may know the hope to which he has called you, the riches of his glorious inheritance in the saints, and his incomparably great power for us who believe. That power is like the working of his mighty strength, which he exerted in Christ when he raised him from the dead and seated him at his right hand in the heavenly realms...(Ephesians 1:18-20).*

We also need to see the potential of our calling: *...far above all rule and authority, power and dominion, and every title that can be given, not only in the present age but also in the one to come. And God placed all things under his feet and appointed him to be head over everything for the church, which is his body, the fullness of him who fills everything in every way (Ephesians 1:21-23).*

And we need to see the position to which he has called us: *And God raised us up with Christ and seated us with him in the heavenly realms in Christ Jesus (Ephesians 2:6).*

After all of this, God has still not convinced Moses that he can do what God has given him: *But Moses said, "O Lord, please send someone else to do it." Then the LORD's anger burned against Moses and he said, "What about your brother, Aaron the Levite? I know he can speak well. He is already on his way to meet you, and his heart will be glad when he sees you. You shall speak to him and put words in his mouth; I will help both of you speak and will teach you what to do. He will speak to the people for you, and it will be as if he were your mouth and as if you were God to him. But take this staff in your hand so you can perform miraculous signs with it" (Ex 4:13-17).*

We've talked about how Moses was never the same after his encounter with God but his time at the burning bush wasn't all positive; it was a mix. Life seems to be a mixture of positive and negative. In my life, I can count as many failures of faith as I can count successes. There are times when I trust God to carry the day and then there are times when I faint and run away. Some days I wake up and say, "Good morning God." Other days it's, "Good God, it's morning." It's encouraging to me to know that it wasn't any different for Moses. As part of his memory of the encounter at the burning bush, he carried with him the knowledge that he let God down that day. It's encouraging to me because God continued to work with Moses in spite of his unbelief. God didn't give up on Moses; neither will God give up on you and me.

In verse 13 Moses isn't refusing to go. He will go if God insists, but he is just asking God if maybe there isn't someone better. Why then did God get so angry? The scripture says God's anger burned! God was angry because above all else what he wants from us is to be believed. He wants us to live by and walk in faith. He wants us to trust him even when it makes no earthly sense.

He wants us to have the kind of faith that his servant Elijah had. Whenever God told Elijah to do something, Elijah did it without question. In Elijah's story, the prophet was in hiding at a place called Kerith, and God told him to go to Zarephath. By all human reasoning there could not have been a worse place to send Elijah. It meant travelling by foot over 100 miles through enemy territory and only to arrive at the enemy's home town in the middle of a famine. Even the name of the place (smelting furnace) didn't sound very inviting. Elijah never questioned his orders. He left immediately for Zarephath. Elijah was wonderfully blessed at Zarephath. God always sends us to a place of blessing.

Are you in the place of blessing? Are you where God wants you today? You know being a person of faith doesn't mean that you never question God, but it also doesn't mean that you only follow him when things make sense. True faith is born in following God into the smelting furnace...following him into a scary place that makes no earthly sense, but following anyway because you trust him.

We are immersing ourselves into Moses' story because we want God to build faith into our lives. We want to be people like Moses who can have great adventures with God. Curiously, here we have an example of a failure of faith for Moses. Now don't misunderstand; Moses wasn't refusing to go. He just wasn't very enthusiastic about the idea. He wasn't convinced that he was the man for the job. So again, why did God get angry with Moses? It's because God likes to be believed. How would God feel if we would just trust him for all the promises he has given us?

So, Jehovah agrees to send Aaron along with Moses. Was this God's first choice? Don't forget it was Aaron who appeased the people one day when Moses was late; he made golden calves and held them up to the people proclaiming, "These are your gods, O Israel, who brought you up out of Egypt." I don't believe Aaron was part of God's "A" plan for Moses. He didn't follow God when it didn't make sense to him, and he had to settle for God's plan B. I wonder how many of us are living God's plan B for our lives, or plan C. Unbelief holds us back. The lesson for us is clear; when God gives you a dream for your life, he will always give you the grace and the power to do the things he gives you to do. *And God is able to make all grace abound to you, so that in all things at all times, having all that you need, you will abound in every good work (2 Corinthians 9:8).* What more do we need?

So the question for us is, how do we come to this place of belief? Do we just grit your teeth and believe? Two stories from scripture give us the answer:

One day a teacher brought his son to Jesus to be healed. Jesus' disciples had already tried to heal the boy and failed. The man asked Jesus, *"If you can do anything, take pity on us and help us."* "If you can?" said Jesus. *"Everything is possible for him who believes" (Mark 9:23).* Look at the amazing response the boy's dad gives Jesus: *Immediately the boy's father exclaimed, "I do believe; help me overcome my unbelief!" (Mark 9:24).* This man asked Jesus to help him believe. One of the things I'm learning about Jesus is that he demands much of us...but everything he demands he gives us. All he really wants from us is to know him, who he is, and what he has done for us. He loves us; he wants us to love him back, and he wants us to follow him. He only needs a small mustard seed of faith from us and he will provide the rest.

Another example is in Matthew: *"Come, follow me,"* *Jesus said, "and I will make you fishers of men" (Matt* *4:19).* Notice that Jesus didn't command his followers to be fishers of men. He commanded only that they follow him. God only asks that we follow him; He will provide everything that we need. *He* *who did not spare his own Son, but gave him up for* *us all--how will he not also, along with him,* *graciously give us all things (Romans 8:32).*

Like Moses, God has a great adventure for each one of us. *You did not choose me, but I chose you and* *appointed you to go and bear fruit--fruit that will* *last. Then the Father will give you whatever you ask* *in my name (John 15:16).*

Moses has spent 40 years in the desert school learning to rely on God for his needs, and it's obvious that he still had some lessons to learn. God was still in the process of bringing Moses to the place of seeing that he was nothing in himself, but with God he had no limits. He was still in the process of opening Moses' eyes so that he would know the hope of his calling.

God is looking for those of us who will follow him today. He's not looking for men and women with talents. He's not looking for people with exceptional courage or intelligence, or even faith. He is simply looking for those who will follow. He wants us to launch out into the danger zone beyond what we can accomplish on our own. He wants us out on a limb where only he can rescue us. I believe that if we pray and ask Jesus, he will begin to work out his dream in each of us. Then as he reveals each step, it is our responsibility to follow and to trust him to do the work. The more we can trust him, the more he can work his plan "A" for us.

CHAPTER 14

The Road Back to Egypt

Then Moses went back to Jethro, his father-in-law, and said to him, "Let me go back to my own people in Egypt to see if any of them are still alive." Jethro said, "Go, and I wish you well" (Ex 4:18). It doesn't sound like Moses shared his burning bush experience with his father-in-law, Jethro. Do you think that maybe when we have deep intimate contact with God that we may be slow to share it with others? Maybe his experience with Jehovah was so intimate and personal that he wanted to keep it to himself.

Now the LORD had said to Moses in Midian, "Go back to Egypt, for all the men who wanted to kill you are dead." So Moses took his wife and sons, put them on a donkey and started back to Egypt. And he took the staff of God in his hand (Ex 4:19-20). Notice that the shepherd's staff is now the staff of God. What belonged to Moses is now God's. Before, the staff was used by Moses for his purposes. Now it is to be used by God for his purposes. Hold onto that thought. And so Moses and his family set out for Egypt.

At a lodging place on the way, the LORD met [Moses] and was about to kill him. But Zipporah took a flint knife, cut off her son's foreskin and touched [Moses'] feet with it. "Surely you are a bridegroom of blood to me," she said. So the LORD let him alone. (At that time she said "bridegroom of blood," referring to circumcision.) (Ex 4:24-26). Whoa! What is going on here? At first these verses seem obscure and weird. What do they mean and why are they here? Let's look closely. *"At a lodging place on the way, the LORD met [Moses] and was about to kill him."* Actually, in the original, this says the Lord "tried" to kill him. Do you see a problem with that? The Lord doesn't "try" to do something. It must be that we are struggling here with the language of what happened. If we were there it would be probably be clearer. My guess is that Moses came down with some very serious sickness, which they interpreted as God trying to kill him. That brings up another question. Why do we sometimes get sick? What are the reasons why we might get sick? (Glory of God, death, learn to trust and rely on God, the fall of man, and sometimes God is just trying to get our attention).

For Moses it is pretty obvious that God wanted to get his attention. One thing we know from the text, is that Moses' son was not circumcised. This was a big deal for a Jew. Without circumcision, an Israelite was cut off from the covenant promises of God. From the text can you guess why Moses' son wasn't circumcised? Moses' wife was a Midianite. The Midianites thought circumcision was disgusting. And so, Moses and Zipporah got the message from God loud and clear. Zipporah performs the rite. Can you tell how happy she is about it?

And so how does all this apply to us? Circumcision is not a part of our spiritual story. *...and you have been given fullness in Christ, who is the head over every power and authority. In him you were also circumcised, in the putting off of the sinful nature, not with a circumcision done by the hands of men but with the circumcision done by Christ, having been buried with him in baptism and raised with him through your faith in the power of God, who raised him from the dead (Colossians 2:10-12).* To the

Israelite, circumcision meant that he had been set aside for God. It separated the Jews from other people and made them God's special possession. Circumcision was a symbolic death to self with a new life now as God's special possession. For us it is no different, but our circumcision is "in Christ." As Christians, we are separated from other people by our position in Christ. Romans 6:4 also says this same thing: *We were therefore buried with him through baptism into death in order that, just as Christ was raised from the dead through the glory of the Father, we too may live a new life.*

Why did all this happen now? Why did God pick this time to deal with Moses about his son? God had commissioned Moses at the burning bush but he wasn't willing to use him until Moses was obedient. This is an important lesson for those of us who want God to use us in a greater way. We've talked about how we want Jesus to teach us to trust him for a great adventure and how it is going to be all about faith and trusting God. Here is where the rubber meets the road. As Christians, we are not subject to the Jewish Law but we are responsible to be obedient to the known will of God. When we begin a great new adventure with God, he is going to start holding us to a higher standard. If you're going to launch out into that danger zone, you are going to have to stay very close to Jesus. When you are in the danger zone, you must follow close or you will lose your way. And so, Moses meets Aaron and together they make their way to Egypt. The adventure begins.

CHAPTER 15

The Front Side of the Desert - Moses Confronts Pharaoh

Okay, Moses is back now on the front side of the desert. He and Aaron go before the people and they tell them everything the Lord had said to Moses and the people believe and bow down to worship Jehovah. What a contrast to the last time Moses tried to get the people to follow his lead. What a difference it makes to have Jehovah go before you. I wonder what Moses was thinking at this point. "This is great; now with God in it this is going to be easy. The people will follow me now, God will deal with Pharaoh, and everything will come up roses from this point on." Moses might have been tempted to indulge in some very wishful thinking. Moses will find that it never gets easy on the great adventure with God. He will find that we must continually trust God for the many giants that will block our path. Moses had to remember, as we must, that the giants we encounter along the adventure path aren't meant to stop us, but to continually keep us dependent on the power of God. Moses was about to meet giant number one – Pharaoh.

Afterward Moses and Aaron went to Pharaoh and said, "This is what the LORD, the God of Israel, says: 'Let my people go, so that they may hold a festival to me in the desert.'" Pharaoh said, "Who is the LORD that I should obey him and let Israel go? I do not know the LORD and I will not let Israel go" (Ex 5:1-2). Remember that as Pharaoh, there were no limits to his power and authority in Egypt. Each Pharaoh was considered a child of the sun and was to be worshipped as a god. The key word in these verses is in verse 2 - "Obey." This was a new concept for Pharaoh who, as a god, obeyed no one. Pharaoh's response to Moses sealed his fate: "I do not know the LORD and I will not let Israel go."

Then they said, "The God of the Hebrews has met with us. Now let us take a three-day journey into the desert to offer sacrifices to the LORD our God, or he may strike us with plagues or with the sword." But the king of Egypt said, "Moses and Aaron, why are you taking the people away from their labor? Get back to your work!" Then Pharaoh said, "Look, the people of the land are now numerous, and you are stopping them from working" (Ex 5:3-5). The battle lines are drawn. Forty years ago it was Moses against Pharaoh. That didn't turn out so well for Moses. Now it is Pharaoh against the God of the Israelites. No contest. Pharaoh was afraid to lose his slave labor. He had a firm grip on them and he would tighten his grip to hold them. It's no different for us today. We have Satan who would hold us in bondage and keep us ineffective in life and ministry and keep us from the great adventure.

Pharaoh vs. Jehovah...no contest. Satan vs. Jesus...no contest (notice that we aren't even in the conflict). *You, dear children, are from God and have overcome them, because the one who is in you is greater than the one who is in the world (1 John 4:4).*

That same day Pharaoh gave this order to the slave drivers and foremen in charge of the people: "You are no longer to supply the people with straw for making bricks; let them go and gather their own straw. But require them to make the same number of bricks as before; don't reduce the quota. They are lazy; that is why they are crying out, 'Let us go and sacrifice to our God.' Make the work harder for the men so that they keep working and pay no attention to lies." (Ex 5:6-9) Why do you think that Pharaoh decided to withhold straw? Was he just being a jerk or was there a plan to his actions? God had ordained a great adventure for the Israelites. He had a new, fresh land for them to conquer and a closer walk with God as they learned to rely on his provision along the way. Pharaoh was playing spoiler. His plan was to get them so miserable in their day-to-day life that they would give up on any grand ideas about their future. Sound familiar? God has ordained a great adventure for each of us. He has a new, fresh land for us to conquer and plans for us to have a closer walk with him as we learn to rely on him for our provision. The Israelites had Pharaoh. We have Satan playing spoiler. His plan is to get us so miserable in our day-to-day lives that we won't have the time, energy, or motivation to pursue the dream that God has for us. How many of us have fallen victim to that?

The Israelite foremen realized they were in trouble when they were told, "You are not to reduce the number of bricks required of you for each day." When they left Pharaoh, they found Moses and Aaron waiting to meet them, and they said, "May the LORD look upon you and judge you! You have made us a stench to Pharaoh and his officials and have put a sword in their hand to kill us"(Ex 5:19-21). Okay, so the Israelites didn't respond too well. It's hard to blame them. But surely Moses wouldn't lose faith. He had spent 40 years preparing for this moment. *Moses returned to the LORD and said, "O Lord, why have you brought trouble upon this people? Is this why you sent me? Ever since I went to Pharaoh to speak in your name, he has brought trouble upon this people, and you have not rescued your people at all"(Ex 5:22-23).*

"you have not rescued your people at all." Let me ask you a question? How can a man who has spent the last 40 years in the desert, schooled by God, a man who has stood at the burning bush and has seen the things that Moses has seen...how can this man now have so little faith? Remember Peter, who could walk on water as long as he was looking at Jesus, but when he took his eyes off Jesus he began to sink. It was the same for Moses, and it's the same for us. When Moses thought about his time at the burning bush and how Jehovah was going to free the Israelites, faith would swell in him. But when he focused on Pharaoh and his unlimited power and authority, then he fainted. The lesson for us is obvious. When we set out on the great adventure

that Jesus will give us, there will be giants along the way.

The giants aren't there to stop us, they are there to demonstrate the power of God on our behalf.

When you set out on the adventure that Jesus will give you, there will be rejection by some. Jesus said they rejected me, they will reject you too. *"If the world hates you, keep in mind that it hated me first. If you belonged to the world, it would love you as its own. As it is, you do not belong to the world, but I have chosen you out of the world. That is why the world hates you. Remember the words I spoke to you: 'No servant is greater than his master.' If they persecuted me, they will persecute you also (John 15:18-20).* The Lord's purpose for us is that we will have peace even as we stand before the giants that block our way: *"I have told you these things, so that in me you may have peace. In this world you will have trouble. But take heart! I have overcome the world"* (John 16:33). There are a few things that we need to hang on to as we face the giants. We must continue in confidence and persevere, trusting Jesus to remove the immovable obstacles.

Also, we must continue with patience because Jesus doesn't always remove the giants on our time table. We must constantly live in the place of trust, always expecting God to come riding to our rescue at the last minute. The Bible tells us to *not become weary in doing good, for at the proper time we will reap a harvest if we do not give up (Gal 6:9).*

Moses was rejected by Pharaoh and then by his own people. He was learning something very valuable. As we said before, these giants don't block our path to stop us, but to show us God at work on our behalf. What did Moses learn from this experience? I think Moses was a man with a deeply ingrained need for the acceptance of others. He was hurt 40 years ago when the people of Israel rejected him, and in returning to Egypt his biggest fear may have been that they would not accept him. Now he is in the place of realizing his greatest fear. Fear can be the biggest giant of all. Fear freezes us into inaction. Fear attacks faith.

Fear will keep you from the great adventure because it causes you to retreat back into your safety zone. God is the God of the impossible. He does not dwell within your safety zone.

Moses was rejected by Pharaoh and then by his own people. He learned something that he was going to need for the rest of his life. He learned what it meant to stand alone with God. The people of Israel weren't great at following and they would rebel over and over in their journey through the wilderness. God had to rip from Moses every vestige of hoping in others so that Moses would have no choice but to stand alone with God. This was a hard lesson for Moses to learn; hard for you and me too.

The Israelite foremen realized they were in trouble when they were told, "You are not to reduce the number of bricks required of you for each day." When they left Pharaoh, they found Moses and Aaron waiting to meet them, and they said, "May the LORD look upon you and judge you! You have made us a stench to Pharaoh and his officials and have put a sword in their hand to kill us." Moses returned to the LORD and said, "O Lord, why have you brought trouble upon this people? Is this why you sent me? Ever since I went to Pharaoh to speak in your name, he has brought trouble upon this people, and you have not rescued your people at all" (Ex 5:19-23). Some very negative things can happen to you on the way to your great adventure. Moses had an enemy (Pharaoh) that would keep him from the calling of God. We also have an enemy. Satan will do all he can to keep us from realizing God's plan for our lives. At times, it may even seem as though the Lord is against us as he allows roadblocks to keep us back. How do we defeat the power of Satan in our lives? How did Moses do it? (Hint - he didn't, Jehovah did.)

Then the LORD said to Moses, "Now you will see what I will do to Pharaoh: Because of my mighty hand he will let them go; because of my mighty hand he will drive them out of his country." (Ex 6:1) Pharaoh was a powerful enemy. Moses had no chance of defeating him, but with God, it was no contest. All Moses had to do was stand and watch as God dealt with Pharaoh. *"Now you will see what I will do to Pharaoh: Because of my mighty hand he will let them go; because of my mighty hand he will drive them out of his country."*

The story of how God delivered Jehoshaphat (another man with another story) perfectly illustrates how to do battle with Satan. In 2 Chronicles chapter 20, a vast army came to make war on Israel and King Jehoshaphat. Alarmed and worried, Jehoshaphat sought the Lord and fasted. Then he gathered all the people together for a prayer meeting. *"O LORD, God of our fathers, are you not the God who is in heaven? You rule over all the kingdoms of the nations. Power and might are in your hand, and no one can withstand you. O our God, did you not drive out the inhabitants of this land before your people Israel and give it forever to the descendants of Abraham your friend? They have lived in it and have built in it a sanctuary for your Name, saying, 'If calamity comes upon us, whether the sword of judgment, or plague or famine, we will stand in your presence before this temple that bears your Name and will cry out to you in our distress, and you will hear us and save us.'* "But now here are men from Ammon, Moab and Mount Seir, whose territory you would not allow Israel to invade when they came from Egypt; so they turned away from them and did not destroy them. See how they are repaying us by coming to drive us out of the possession you gave us as an inheritance. O our God, will you not judge them? For we have no power to face this vast army that is attacking us. We do not know what to do, but our eyes are upon you" *(2 Chron 20:6-12).* The Lord sent a prophet to give them his answer to their prayers: He said: *Listen King Jehoshaphat and all who live in Judah and Jerusalem! This is what the LORD says to you: "Do not be afraid or discouraged because of this vast army. For the battle is not yours, but God's. Tomorrow march down against them. They will be climbing up by the Pass of Ziz, and you will find them at the end of the gorge in the Desert of Jeruel. You will not have to fight this battle. Take up your positions; stand firm and see the deliverance the LORD will give you, O Judah and Jerusalem. Do not be afraid; do not be discouraged. Go out to face them tomorrow, and the LORD will be with you" (2 Chron 20:15-17).*

As we stand with God, he will sweep away our enemy as he did Jehoshaphat's enemy and as he did Pharaoh. But Pharaoh wasn't the only giant blocking the way. Moses also had to learn how to handle his inner demons. Why have the people rejected me? What if they won't follow me? Moses' biggest giant was fear of rejection. You may have a similar giant or yours may be unique. Anything that smacks of fear of men or a feeling of inadequacy fits into this category. God's word has an answer for that too: *God also said to Moses, "I am the LORD. I appeared to Abraham, to Isaac and to Jacob as God Almighty, but by my name the LORD I did not make myself known to them. I also established my covenant with them to give them the land of Canaan, where they lived as aliens. Moreover, I have heard the groaning of the Israelites, whom the Egyptians are enslaving, and I have remembered my covenant (Ex 6:2-5).* The Lord said it's not about you Moses; it's not your dream, it's my dream. I'm the one who has heard the groaning of my people and I am the one who will rescue them. You see the great adventure isn't about going out and changing the world; the great adventure is tagging along with Jesus as he changes the world. This thought has been very freeing for me. I am not responsible for results when I am ministering to others. If I am ministering at God's direction, I can just rest in Jesus and watch him work. I *"...have stilled and quieted my soul; like a weaned child with its mother, like a weaned child is my soul within me" (Ps 131:2).*

CHAPTER 16

Pharaoh's Heart is Hardened

So God has a plan to bring plagues upon Egypt until Pharaoh allows the Jews to go. First, there are nine plagues that only serve to harden Pharaoh's resolve to not let them go; one final plague breaks Pharaoh's stubbornness. I've always wondered about these plagues. If God knew (and of course he did), that the first nine plagues wouldn't get the job done, why bring them? It makes me think that just maybe God had more reasons for the plagues than a seemingly desperate bid to convince Pharaoh. There are several other reasons why God may have brought the plagues. First, the plagues revealed God's mighty power and that he was greater than any of the so-called gods of Egypt. I wonder if some of the Egyptian people became believers during this time. Second, the plagues may have been meant to progressively break down Pharaoh's stubbornness. Third, the plagues served to strengthen the faith of Moses. Fourth, they also served to encourage and strengthen the faith of the Israelite people. And so, the nine plagues hit Egypt with progressive intensity. First, there was a plague of blood where Moses struck the water of the Nile River with the staff and all the water in all of Egypt turned to blood (Ex 7:14-25). Then seven days later he brought a plague of frogs (Ex 8:1-11), then a plague of lice (Ex 8:12-15), then flies (Ex 8:20-32). Then he brought an epidemic among the livestock (Ex 9:1-7), then boils (Ex 9:8-12), then hail (Ex 9:13-35), then locusts (Ex 10:1-20). The ninth plague was a plague of darkness (Ex 10-21-29).

CHAPTER 17

_____

The 10th and Final Plague

Now the LORD had said to Moses, "I will bring one more plague on Pharaoh and on Egypt. After that, he will let you go from here, and when he does, he will drive you out completely. Tell the people that men and women alike are to ask their neighbors for articles of silver and gold." (The LORD made the Egyptians favorably disposed toward the people, and Moses himself was highly regarded in Egypt by Pharaoh's officials and by the people). So Moses said, "This is what the LORD says: 'About midnight I will go throughout Egypt. Every firstborn son in Egypt will die, from the firstborn son of Pharaoh, who sits on the throne, to the firstborn son of the slave girl, who is at her hand mill, and all the firstborn of the cattle as well. There will be loud wailing throughout Egypt-- worse than there has ever been or ever will be again. But among the Israelites not a dog will bark at any man or animal.' Then you will know that the LORD makes a distinction between Egypt and Israel. All these officials of yours will come to me, bowing down before me and saying, 'Go, you and all the people who follow you!' After that I will leave." Then Moses, hot with anger, left Pharaoh. The LORD had said to Moses, "Pharaoh will refuse to listen to you--so that my wonders may be multiplied in Egypt." Moses and Aaron performed all these wonders before Pharaoh, but the LORD hardened Pharaoh's heart, and he would not let the Israelites go out of his country. The LORD said to Moses and Aaron in Egypt, "This month is to be for you the first month, the first month of your year. Tell the whole community of Israel that on the tenth day of this month each man is to take a lamb for his family, one for each household. If any household is too small for a whole lamb, they must share one with their nearest neighbor, having taken into account the number of people there are. You are to determine the amount of lamb needed in accordance with what each person will eat. The animals you choose must be year-old males without defect, and you may take them from the sheep or the goats. Take care of them until the fourteenth day of the month, when all the people of the community of Israel must slaughter them at twilight. Then they are to take some of the blood and put it on the sides and tops of the doorframes of the houses where they eat the lambs. That same night they are to eat the meat roasted over the fire, along with bitter herbs, and bread made without yeast. Do not eat the meat raw or cooked in water, but roast it over the fire--head, legs and inner parts. Do not leave any of it till morning; if some is left till morning, you must burn it. This is how you are to eat it: with your cloak tucked into your belt, your sandals on your feet and your staff in your hand. Eat it in haste; it is the LORD's Passover. "On that same night I will pass through Egypt and strike down every firstborn--both men and animals--and I will bring judgment on all the gods of Egypt. I am the LORD. The blood will be a sign for you on the houses where you are; and when I see the blood, I will pass over you. No destructive plague will touch you when I strike Egypt (Ex 11:10-12:13). For the Egyptians it was a final and terrible plague. For the Israelites it was a new beginning. They had entered Egypt as a family - they leave as a great nation blessed by God.

What was the purpose of putting blood on the sides and top of the doors? What would happen to an

Israelite family if they didn't put blood on the door? What if a family simply put a sign on their door that said they were Jews, they trusted God, and that they knew that he was loving and merciful and not the kind of God that would kill them? Wouldn't that be good enough? What's the deal with all the blood? *For the life of a creature is in the blood, and I have given it to you to make atonement for yourselves on the altar; it is the blood that makes atonement for one's life (Leviticus 17:11). In fact, the law requires that nearly everything be cleansed with blood, and without the shedding of blood there is no forgiveness (Hebrews 9:22).*

The Israelites were not going to escape the judgment of the killing of the firstborn on their own merit, but on the merit of the blood applied to the doorposts. No matter how reasonable some other method may have seemed, only blood on the doorposts would save them. The blood on the doorposts and then later the Old Testament Passover was of course, a picture of the salvation that was to come. It looked forward to the time when Christ would shed his blood for sins of the whole world. The shed blood of the lamb on the doorposts saved the Israelites. The shed blood of the Lamb of God (Jesus) saves us. *He is the atoning sacrifice for our sins, and not only for ours but also for the sins of the whole world (1 John 2:2).*

Just like the shed blood of the lamb was the only way for the Israelites to be saved, so the blood of Jesus is the only way for us. *For you know that it was not with perishable things such as silver or gold that you were redeemed from the empty way of life handed down to you from your forefathers, but with the precious blood of Christ, a lamb without blemish or defect (1 Peter 1:18-19).*

There are many today that try to stand on their own merit or perception of God to save them, but it will not. There are many today who think that all beliefs are equally good, but that is a lie. Truth is not subjective. There is only one truth, only one true God. There is one promise: *"I tell you the truth, whoever hears my word and believes him who sent me has eternal life and will not be condemned; he has crossed over from death to life (John 5:24).*

Then Moses summoned all the elders of Israel and said to them, "Go at once and select the animals for your families and slaughter the Passover lamb. Take a bunch of hyssop, dip it into the blood in the basin and put some of the blood on the top and on both sides of the doorframe. Not one of you shall go out the door of his house until morning. When the LORD goes through the land to strike down the Egyptians, he will see the blood on the top and sides of the doorframe and will pass over that doorway, and he will not permit the destroyer to enter your houses and strike you down. Obey these instructions as a lasting ordinance for you and your descendants. When you enter the land that the LORD will give you as he promised, observe this ceremony. And when your children ask you, 'What does this ceremony mean to you?' then tell them, 'It is the Passover sacrifice to the LORD, who passed over the houses of the Israelites in Egypt and spared our homes when he struck down the Egyptians.'" Then the people bowed down and worshiped. The Israelites did just what the LORD commanded Moses and Aaron (Ex 12:21-28). Before the first nine plagues, the Israelites were upset with Moses for getting Pharaoh angry at them and increasing their work load. What a difference a plague makes. *At midnight the LORD struck down all the firstborn in Egypt, from the firstborn of Pharaoh, who sat on the throne, to the firstborn of the prisoner, who was in the dungeon, and the firstborn of all the livestock as well. Pharaoh and all his officials and all the Egyptians got up during the night, and there was loud wailing in Egypt, for there was not a house without someone dead (Ex 12:29-30).*

CHAPTER 18

Out of Egypt

During the night Pharaoh summoned Moses and Aaron and said, "Up! Leave my people, you and the Israelites! Go, worship the LORD as you have requested. Take your flocks and herds, as you have said, and go. And also bless me" (Ex 12:31-32). He brought out Israel, laden with silver and gold, and from among their tribes no one faltered. Egypt was glad when they left, because dread of Israel had fallen on them (Psalms 105:37-38). And so the Israelites left Egypt. They may have left with great joy, but it wouldn't be long before Jehovah would test their faith. He always wants us to know if we will trust him and follow him into places that make no sense.

When they left Egypt, they could have gone straight north and followed the Mediterranean Sea; they could have been in Canaan in just a matter of days. But the Lord led them east into the desert. Why did God lead them the wrong way? *When Pharaoh let the people go, God did not lead them on the road through the Philistine country, though that was shorter. For God said, "If they face war, they might change their minds and return to Egypt." So God led the people around by the desert road toward the Red Sea. The Israelites went up out of Egypt armed for battle...By day the LORD went ahead of them in a pillar of cloud to guide them on their way and by night in a pillar of fire to give them light, so that they could travel by day or night. Neither the pillar of cloud by day nor the pillar of fire by night left its place in front of the people (Ex 13:17-18,21-22).*

And so the Israelites left Egypt filled with faith and trusting their God to lead them to their promised land. Jehovah seldom takes us on a direct route. He uses the circumstances of an indirect route to build our faith. The Israelite's faith at this point was shallow and easily shattered.

CHAPTER 19

Deliverance at the Red Sea

Let's set the scene for what happens next: *When the king of Egypt was told that the people had fled, Pharaoh and his officials changed their minds about them and said, "What have we done? We have let the Israelites go and have lost their services!" So he had his chariot made ready and took his army with him. He took six hundred of the best chariots, along with all the other chariots of Egypt, with officers over all of them. The LORD hardened the heart of Pharaoh King of Egypt, so that he pursued the Israelites, who were marching out boldly. The Egyptians--all Pharaoh's horses and chariots, horsemen and troops--pursued the Israelites and overtook them as they camped by the sea near Pi Hahiroth, opposite Baal Zephon (Exodus 14:5-9).* The Israelites marched out boldly, but they hadn't yet attended the desert school and their faith was weak and fragile. As soon as trouble reared its ugly head, their confidence folded like a cheap tent in a sandstorm. *As Pharaoh approached, the Israelites looked up, and there were the Egyptians, marching after them. They were terrified and cried out to the LORD. They said to Moses, "Was it because there were no graves in Egypt that you brought us to the desert to die? What have you done to us by bringing us out of Egypt? Didn't we say to you in Egypt, 'Leave us alone; let us serve the Egyptians? It would have been better for us to serve the Egyptians than to die in the desert!'" (Ex 14:10-12).*

The Lord provided a pillar of cloud during the day and a pillar of fire at night to guide them. Wouldn't you think that would be enough to encourage them that God was with them and would protect them? The Israelites were hemmed in on all sides. On one side they had an impassible mountain range. On the other side were vast sand dunes that could not be crossed on foot. In front of them was the Red Sea and behind them the pursuing Egyptian army. They were trapped. Their morale sank. This was their first real test as a nation. But their problem wasn't

Pharaoh. Their problem was that they couldn't see Jehovah working in their circumstances. The Bible is full of stories where God's men and women were faced with impossible circumstances. The solution for every one of them was never the size of their army but rather the size of their God. One morning the Prophet Elisha's servant went out of his tent to see a vast army surrounding the city. Running to his master he exclaimed, *"Oh lord, what shall we do?"* True to all of God's giants of faith, Elisha answered his servant, *"Don't be afraid,"* ... *"Those who are with us are more than those who are with them." And Elisha prayed, "O LORD, open his eyes so he may see." Then the LORD opened the servant's eyes, and he looked and saw the hills full of horses and chariots of fire all around Elisha (2 Kings 6:16-17).*

The Israelites' faith was weak. The Lord would spend many years building their faith. Some of them would respond, others would not. The Lord had designed a special school of the desert for them just as he had for Moses. Isn't it interesting that the Lord uses the desert times of our lives to teach us to trust him for our needs. Some of us respond by crying out to God and throwing ourselves into his arms. Others respond by becoming bitter and blaming God or those around them for their unmet needs.

Now Moses' response to the impossible situation was different than that of the people. He had already spent 40 years in the school of the desert and he had stood before the burning bush. All of Moses' training with Jehovah was for such a time as this. Moses answered the people, "*Do not be afraid. Stand firm and you will see the deliverance the LORD will bring you today. The Egyptians you see today you will never see again. The LORD will fight for you; you need only to be still*" *(Ex 14:13-14).* Consider the three commands in Moses' statement. The first command was "fear not!" Israel was completely hemmed in with a fierce Egyptian army on its way, and yet he said-- "fear not." What was the source of Moses' confidence? Was it the old Moses who would rally the Israelites to fight a fierce battle with the Egyptians, or was it the new Moses with confidence in the hand of God? The Lord wants us to learn to lean on him in the scary times. Consider Abraham. God's word to him as he faced an uncertain future was *Do not be afraid, Abram. I am your shield, your very great reward (Gen 15:1).* Joshua lost confidence after the Israelites' defeat at Ai - *Then the LORD said to Joshua, "Do not be afraid; do not be discouraged. Take the whole army with you, and go up and attack Ai. For I have delivered into your hands the king of Ai, his people, his city and his land" (Joshua 8:1).* Gideon was afraid for his life when the Midianites invaded Israel - *But the LORD said to him, "Peace! Do not be afraid. You are not going to die" (Judges 6:23).*

Isaiah summed this all up: *You will keep in perfect peace him whose mind is steadfast, because he trusts in you. Trust in the LORD forever, for the LORD, the LORD, is the Rock eternal (Isaiah 26:3-4).*

Moses' second command to the people was to "stand firm." Sometimes the hardest thing to do is nothing. It's hard to wait. We think we have to do something. Faith, though, isn't about solving the problem. Faith is about rising above the problem to the throne of God.

Thirdly, Moses said "see." *See the deliverance the LORD will bring you today.* Think of how helpless the Israelites were. They couldn't dry up the Red Sea. They couldn't level the mountains or bridge the impassable sand. They couldn't annihilate the armies of Egypt. They were in a completely impossible situation. The good news was that they were in the exact place where the Lord loves to work.

The Lord delights in leading us into impossible circumstances and then displaying his grace and power on our behalf.

Then the LORD said to Moses, "Why are you crying out to me? Tell the Israelites to move on. Raise your staff and stretch out your hand over the sea to divide the water so that the Israelites can go through the sea on dry ground. I will harden the hearts of the Egyptians so that they will go in after them. And I will gain glory through Pharaoh and all his army, through his chariots and his horsemen. The Egyptians will know that I am the LORD when I gain glory through Pharaoh, his chariots and his horsemen." Then the angel of God, who had been traveling in front of Israel's army, withdrew and went behind them. The pillar of cloud also moved from in front and stood behind them, coming between the armies of Egypt and Israel. Throughout the night the cloud brought darkness to the one side and light to the other side; so neither went near the other all night long. Then Moses stretched out his hand over the sea, and all that night the LORD drove the sea back with a strong east wind and turned it into dry land. The waters were divided, and the Israelites went through the sea on dry ground, with a wall of water on their right and on their left. The Egyptians pursued them, and all Pharaoh's horses, chariots and horsemen followed them into the sea. During the last watch of the night the LORD looked down from the pillar of fire and cloud at the Egyptian army and threw it into confusion. He made the wheels of their chariots come off so that they had difficulty driving. And the Egyptians said, "Let's get away from the Israelites! The LORD is fighting for them against Egypt." Then the LORD said to Moses, "Stretch out your hand over the sea so that the waters may flow back over the Egyptians and their chariots and horsemen." Moses stretched out his hand over the sea, and at daybreak the sea went back to its place. The Egyptians were fleeing toward it, and the LORD swept them into the sea. The water flowed back and covered the chariots and horsemen--the entire army of Pharaoh that had followed the Israelites into the sea. Not one of them survived. But the Israelites went through the sea on dry ground, with a wall of water on their right and on their left. That day the LORD saved Israel from the hands of the Egyptians, and Israel saw the Egyptians lying dead on the shore. And when the Israelites saw the great power the LORD displayed against the Egyptians, the people feared the LORD and put their trust in him and in Moses his servant (Ex 14:15-31).

The people feared the Lord and put their trust in him. Real faith would have been to trust God on the other side of the Red Sea. But now Israel's deliverance from Egypt was complete, just as God had promised 400 years before. When the water flowed back and covered the Egyptian army, the Lord had kept his word. The power of Egypt was broken forever. Egypt lived on, but Egypt as a world-wide power would never rise again. When God broke the power of Egypt, he painted a picture of how someday he would break the power of Satan. The power of Egypt was broken forever at the Red Sea even though it lived on. The power of Satan was broken at the Cross of Christ even though Satan lives on to tempt and condemn us.

CHAPTER 20

_____

Potholes on the Road to Canaan

The Israelites were ecstatic. After generations in captivity, they were now free. They were free and their faith in Jehovah God was renewed. They left Egypt filled with faith and ready for new adventures. The Lord knew though that their faith was weak and fragile. That's why he led them on the "long road." *When Pharaoh let the people go, God did not lead them on the road through the Philistine country, though that was shorter. For God said, "If they face war, they might change their minds and return to Egypt." So God led the people around by the desert road toward the Red Sea (Ex 13:17-18).* They could have been in Canaan in a short time, but God led them on a path that would take them several years. He had spent the last 40 years working on their leader, but the Israelites still needed to learn to trust him. God knew that even though they were excited and anxious to follow him, their faith was weak and wouldn't hold up to severe testing. And so, they set off on the long road to the Promised Land and a series of trials meant to build their faith.

Then Moses led Israel from the Red Sea and they went into the Desert of Shur. For three days they traveled in the desert without finding water. When they came to Marah, they could not drink its water because it was bitter. (That is why the place is called Marah). So the people grumbled against Moses, saying, "What are we to drink?" (Ex 15:22-24). Can you believe it? Three days after singing and dancing and praising the Lord for delivering them at the Red Sea, and they have completely lost it over some bitter water. Of course, you and I know that this setback was not meant to stop them but to show them that God didn't just send them toward Canaan but that he intended to be with them every step of the way. This obstacle was meant to help strengthen their faith; you and I recognize that. Does it seem strange to you that the Israelites didn't "get it" and go immediately to prayer rather than yell at Moses? What about you and me? Do we "get it" when we come to the place called Marah? Do we cry out to God when we come across the bitter water in our lives, or do we look for someone to blame? Why, Lord, do we see it so clearly in others but miss it in our own lives? *Then Moses cried out to the Lord, and the Lord showed him a piece of wood. He threw it into the water, and the water became sweet (Ex 15:25).*

About six weeks after leaving Egypt, the Israelites came to their next time of crisis: *The whole Israelite community set out from Elim and came to the Desert of Sin, which is between Elim and Sinai, on the fifteenth day of the second month after they had come out of Egypt. In the desert the whole community grumbled against Moses and Aaron. The Israelites said to them, "If only we had died by the Lord's hand in Egypt! There we sat around pots of meat and ate all the food we wanted, but you have brought us out into this desert to starve this entire assembly to death" (Ex 16:1-3).* I don't know what to say. Some of us are just slow learners. This was just another trial to show them that they had not been forgotten as they traveled the dusty road, but that the God who called them out of Egypt was the God who was committed to take care of them. Do you have a sense in your life that the God who called you out of the world and into his family is committed to take care of you? If you don't really have that assurance in your life, you may have more desert roads yet to travel. God showed himself faithful to the Israelites with manna and quail to eat. He can take care of you too. The "Bread of Heaven" is not in short supply.

Over and over again the Lord would test them. They ran out of water several more times and each time the Lord provided a miracle to strengthen them. The Lord appeared to them in a dense cloud at Mount Sinai and through Moses he gave them laws to obey; all designed to help them know him and put their complete trust in only him. For us, we need to begin to see the negative trials that come into our lives as an opportunity to practice faith and trust. Instead of a dense cloud, we have God's Word and the Holy Spirit that we might know him and trust him.

CHAPTER 21

Kadesh Barnea: Gateway to Promise or Waterloo

We have seen that Moses' story is also our story. As Moses was slowly brought from faith to faith, so God also works in us to bring us to the place of trust. A study of Israel's history also reveals many parallels that can be drawn to the individual believer today. This is especially true of Israel's travels from Egypt to Canaan. As Israel came out of Egyptian captivity, passed through the wilderness, and eventually entered the Promised Land, God painted a picture for us of the spiritual journey we go through as we learn to trust God for our lives.

The Jews in Egypt are symbolic of our lives before we knew Jesus. We were all born in Egypt. In Egypt they ate leeks and onions, strong food that to us represents the worldliness and materialistic natures that we were all born into. Every one of us was born with a "he who dies with the most toys wins" mentality. Every one of us was born selfish and self-centered. Every one of us was born in slavery. The wilderness represents our journey from selfishness to selflessness, the path from godlessness to godliness, the adventure from living in slavery to living in the heavenlies with Christ. Canaan does not represent heaven as incorrectly portrayed by some of our music, but rather represents our lives as mature Christians. Canaan life is a life of spiritual warfare and conquest as we claim the freedom land that God has promised us and gone ahead to secure for us. The road to Canaan is the road to faith. The Israelites left Egypt, delivered by the blood of the first born. God separated Israel from Egypt at the Red Sea, provided for them in the desert with a cloud to guide them, manna to eat, water to drink, and protection from their enemies. God spent two years leading his people and teaching them to rely on him for their needs and to trust him with their future. After those two years, the people came to the desert of Paran to a place called Kadesh Barnea. Kadesh

Barnea was a gateway to Canaan...the Promised Land, the land that God had reserved for the descendants of Abraham. For them Kadesh Barnea was a place of decision. Would they trust God to make good on his promise or would they see the obstacles in the way and shrink back. Would Kadesh Barnea be the gateway to promise or would it be their Waterloo?

As believers, we stand on the basis of our position in Christ, delivered by the blood of the first born. Our lives are supposed to be characterized as abundant and victorious. If your life isn't abundant and victorious, you may be still in the desert. In fact, you may be at Kadesh Barnea today...the place of decision. Are you going to trust God and what he can do with your life; are you going to move into his promises today, or are you stuck with only your own resources to fall back on? Are you going to trust the God of the impossible today or are you going to shrink back from the victorious Christian life that he intends for you because the giants are too big?

After that, the people left Hazeroth and encamped in the Desert of Paran. The Lord said to Moses, "Send some men to explore the land of Canaan, which I am giving to the Israelites. From each ancestral tribe send one of its leaders"(Numbers 12:16-13:2). The

Lord had Moses send leaders from each of the twelve tribes. Moses probably spent personal time with each leader. They would have known God's plan and would have witnessed all the times that God had protected them and cared for them in the wilderness. If Moses could count on anyone to operate in faith as they scouted out the land, it should have been these men.

Read Numbers 12:16 again. Whose idea was it to send spies to check out the land? It reads as though it was God's idea doesn't it? But think, why would God have them send spies? God already knew what they would see, and what does sending spies have to do with walking by faith? Could it be that it was their idea and God was merely allowing it, even though it wasn't His "best" for them? Check out the same scene from the book of Deuteronomy: *Then, as the LORD our God commanded us, we set out from Horeb and went toward the hill country of the Amorites through all that vast and dreadful desert that you have seen, and so we reached Kadesh Barnea. Then I said to you, "You have reached the hill country of the Amorites, which the LORD our God is giving us. See, the LORD your God has given you the land. Go up and take possession of it as the LORD, the God of your fathers, told you. Do not be afraid; do not be discouraged." Then all of you came to me and said,*

"Let us send men ahead to spy out the land for us and bring back a report about the route we are to take and the towns we will come to." The idea seemed good to me; so I selected twelve of you, one man from each tribe (Deut 1:19-23). God never intended for them to send spies. His first choice was that they just trust him to take care of them and enter the land. This single act of mistrust would start a chain of events, and except for two people, none of the adults alive at this time would ever enter the land. God sometimes gives us what we pray for instead of his best for us. This is a real lesson for us, to pray in an attitude of submission where his will always comes first. God knows what is best for us and he sees our future. It's important for us to have a mindset where we are always ready to launch out at his command.

Jesus gives us an example of what it means to always defer to God rather than our own thoughts or desires: *Going a little farther, he fell with his face to the ground and prayed, "My Father, if it is possible, may this cup be taken from me. Yet not as I will, but as you will" (Matt 26:39).*

In numbers 13:14-15, Moses gives us the names of each leader that was sent in to check out the land. Their names were Shammua, Shaphat, Caleb, Igal,

Hohsea (Joshua), Palti, Gaddiel, Gaddi, Ammiel, Sethur, Hahbi, and Geuel. I'll tell you later why I wanted us to read the list of leaders that Moses sent in to spy the land. Names were important to the Jews. Notice that Joshua was originally named Hohsea, which means, "to play it safe." After he got back from spying out the land and gave his report, Moses changed his name to Joshua, which means "savior." Maybe God has a new name for you!

And so the spies entered the land and returned to Moses with their report: *They gave Moses this account: "We went into the land to which you sent us, and it does flow with milk and honey! Here is its fruit. But the people who live there are powerful, and the cities are fortified and very large. We even saw descendants of Anak there. The Amalekites live in the Negev; the Hittites, Jebusites and Amorites live in the hill country; and the Canaanites live near the sea and along the Jordan." Then Caleb silenced the people before Moses and said, "We should go up and take possession of the land, for we can certainly do it" (Num 13:27-30).* I am glad my grandson is named Caleb; I pray he lives up to his namesake. *But the men who had gone up with him said, "We can't attack those people; they are stronger than we are." And they spread among the Israelites a bad report about the land they had explored. They said, "The*

*land we explored devours those living in it. All the
people we saw there are of great size. We saw the
Nephilim there (the descendants of Anak come from
the Nephilim). We seemed like grasshoppers in our
own eyes, and we looked the same to them" (Num
13:31-33).*

Do you always have to be positive? Is it wrong to be
against a particular plan? Why was it wrong for these
guys? *That night all the people of the community
raised their voices and wept aloud. All the Israelites
grumbled against Moses and Aaron, and the whole
assembly said to them, "If only we had died in Egypt!
Or in this desert! Why is the LORD bringing us to this
land only to let us fall by the sword? Our wives and
children will be taken as plunder. Wouldn't it be
better for us to go back to Egypt?" (Num 14:1-3).* The
root of what they were saying was that they didn't
trust the Lord. They had sent spies to check out the
land because they didn't trust him, and now that
they had seen the giants in the land they didn't trust
him to help them conquer them.

Moses and Aaron fall facedown at the news. Joshua
and Caleb plead with the people to trust God: *And
they said to each other, "We should choose a leader
and go back to Egypt." Then Moses and Aaron fell
facedown in front of the whole Israelite assembly*

gathered there. Joshua son of Nun and Caleb son of Jephunneh, who were among those who had explored the land, tore their clothes and said to the entire Israelite assembly, "The land we passed through and explored is exceedingly good. If the LORD is pleased with us, he will lead us into that land, a land flowing with milk and honey, and will give it to us. Only do not rebel against the LORD. And do not be afraid of the people of the land, because we will swallow them up. Their protection is gone, but the LORD is with us. Do not be afraid of them." But the whole assembly talked about stoning them. Then the glory of the LORD appeared at the Tent of Meeting to all the Israelites. The LORD said to Moses, "How long will these people treat me with contempt? How long will they refuse to believe in me, in spite of all the miraculous signs I have performed among them?" (Num 14:4-11).

How do you suppose God was feeling? *How long will these people treat me with contempt? How long will they refuse to believe in me…"* God knew the difficulties that the Israelites would face when they entered the land. He could have wiped the previous inhabitants of the land from the face of the earth with a single thought, but he would rather have the Israelites do it in his power as they learned to trust in his presence. He promised them that he would be with them. Instead of moving out confident of his presence, they shrunk back and seemed like grasshoppers in their own eyes. They had forgotten the Lord's word to them in Egypt: *"I will bring you to the land I swore with uplifted hand to give to Abraham, to Isaac and to Jacob. I will give it to you as a possession. I am the LORD'"* (Ex 6:8).

God's response to their unbelief was: *I will strike them down with a plague and destroy them...(Num 14:12).* Moses pleads with God for the people: *If you put these people to death all at one time, the nations who have heard this report about you will say, "The LORD was not able to bring these people into the land he promised them on oath; so he slaughtered them in the desert"* (Num 14:15-16). Now don't misunderstand this exchange between Moses and Jehovah. At first glance it looks like God is ready to nuke the whole bunch of them. He even told Moses that after they were dead he would make a great nation from Moses' seed. Does that mean he is going back on his promise to Abraham to bless his descendants? It looks like Moses has the wiser argument here, but we know that can't be true. So, what really is happening here? I believe this was one more test for Moses. The Lord was training him not just to live by faith, but also to be a wise leader for the people. I think Moses passed this test with flying colors. Notice that Moses was more interested in protecting God's reputation than he was in being promoted. You live your life labeled with the word "Christian." Do your words and your actions show your concern for Christ's reputation?

The LORD replied, "I have forgiven them, as you asked. Nevertheless, as surely as I live and as surely as the glory of the LORD fills the whole earth, not one of the men who saw my glory and the miraculous signs I performed in Egypt and in the desert but who disobeyed me and tested me ten times-- not one of them will ever see the land I promised on oath to their forefathers. No one who has treated me with contempt will ever see it. But because my servant Caleb has a different spirit and follows me wholeheartedly, I will bring him into the land he went to, and his descendants will inherit it (Num 14:20-24). We read the names of the other 10 men who went to spy out the land because their names aren't found anywhere else in the Bible. They are only known for their unbelief. Here lies Shammua, he could have entered the land, slain giants, feasted on the fruits, conquered in the name of his God...but he didn't believe. Our God is the same God that Israel had. They did not believe in God's willingness and ability to enable them to overcome the obstacles they would encounter on the way. Are we? Are we ready to move from the place where we are and go on to do great things for God in His strength, or are we limited to only what WE can do?

Are we going to take God at his word or are we going to check out the reasonableness of his promises? God could have just made earth a heaven for us and wiped out our enemies, but this place isn't meant to be heaven. Here is where God wants to change you into the likeness of his son. Here is where he wants to prepare you for an eternity with him. He isn't going to wipe out your enemies, but today he gives you the same promise he gave the Israelites: *"...I am the LORD, and I will bring you out from under the yoke of the Egyptians. I will free you from being slaves to them, and I will redeem you with an outstretched arm and with mighty acts of judgment. I will take you as my own people, and I will be your God. Then you will know that I am the LORD your God, who brought you out from under the yoke of the Egyptians. And I will bring you to the land I swore with uplifted hand to give to Abraham, to Isaac and to Jacob. I will give it to you as a possession. I am the LORD'" (Ex 6:6-8).*

What are the giants in your life that bar the way to the freedom in Christ that God has secured for you? What are the giants in your life that keep you from possessing the land, from being the triumphant Christian that God made you to be? What are the giants in your life that hold you back? How big are the giants? How big is your God? *What, then, shall we say in response to this? If God is for us, who can be against us? He who did not spare his own Son, but gave him up for us all-- how will he not also, along with him, graciously give us all things? (Rom 8:31-32). You, dear children, are from God and have overcome them, because the one who is in you is greater than the one who is in the world (1 John 4:4).*

The lesson from Kadesh Barnea: *We live by faith, not by sight (2 Cor 5:7).*

CHAPTER 22

———————————

The Healing Metaphor

Fast forward 40 years. Led by Moses, Aaron and their sister Miriam, Israel has been wandering in the desert all these years since their failure of faith at Kadesh Barnea. They literally went in circles covering the same ground over and over again. It was an accurate picture of the life many of us lead. Having failed to believe God's plan for our life we wander through this life desperately looking for what will satisfy. God made each of us and he made us with a plan and for a purpose. We were made for God's purpose and we can never be satisfied except when our lives are fulfilling that purpose. Many today feel this sense of unfulfillment and they desperately search to find meaning in life. You can see it all around you. There are those that search for it in money, or career, or relationships. Some have given up seeking and instead just try to escape the emptiness in distractions like alcohol or drugs. Some think that possessions will satisfy, but they quickly find that the joy of owning is short and fleeting. The truth is that you were made for a purpose and you will never be satisfied with any life that isn't fulfilling that purpose. The path to joy is finding who you are in Christ.

Having missed God's purpose for their lives, the Israelites wandered the land hopeless and lost. As the years went by and the Israelites died off one by one, those remaining got increasingly bitter and discouraged. Even though Jehovah met all of their needs in the wilderness, they never came to the place of trust and rest. As they died off, God's agenda turned to their children. For the children, the desert experience became a place of training just as it had for Moses all those years before. It was in this desert wandering that God began to bring them tests to build their faith. Let's check in with them as their 40-year desert school is coming to a close.

They traveled from Mount Hor along the route to the Red Sea, to go around Edom (Num 21:4). The

Edomites are the children of Esau, Jacob's son. The Lord told the Israelites, "You go around Edom. You are not to lay a hand on those Edomites because they too are my children." This is just a side note, but did you know that the Muslim nations are also children of Abraham, and God loves them just like he loved these Edomites. God loves the Muslim people. With all of the terrorism today, if you find yourself hating Muslims, you should re-evaluate.

But the people grew impatient on the way; they spoke against God and against Moses, and said, "Why have you brought us up out of Egypt to die in the desert? There is no bread! There is no water! And we detest this miserable food!" (Numbers 21:4-5). The people got discouraged and started to complain. As Yogi Berra said, "It's déjà vu all over again. It seems that the Israelites went through the desert traveling from one pity party to the next and never learning to just trust. For 40 years this generation has been burying their parents behind them. For 40 years they've been slogging through the burning sands. Over all these years it seems that they have developed a collective negative spirit. Have you ever noticed that when you meet someone with a negative spirit you can often trace it back to a parent with a negative spirit? Like father like son, like mother like daughter. These Israelite kids came by it naturally. Mom and Dad sat across the supper table at night and ripped on Moses and Aaron and even Jehovah. Their negativity when the spies came back after scoping out the Promised Land had cost them their right to cross over and doomed them to die in this desert, and now the negativity was infecting the kids. A negative spirit is highly contagious. Guard yourself against a negative spirit. It's easy to catch but hard to get rid of.

And so the people are complaining to Moses and Aaron. "Hey Moses, come on now. This manna wasn't that bad, but we've been eating it for 40 years. I just gag now when I see manna these days." Forty years on the same diet. Wouldn't you get sick of it? I would. But I have to remind you that this wasn't God's plan. He never intended that they would be walking around in circles in the desert for 40 years. His plan for them was that they would go straight into the Promised Land, but because of their unbelief, they've been stuck with that bread for all these years. They can't blame Moses and they can't blame God for these 40 years. We also can't blame God because we are stuck with the consequences of our own poor choices or our own failure to answer his call to faith.

They spoke against God and against Moses, and said, "Why have you brought us up out of Egypt to die in the desert? There is no bread! There is no water! And we detest this miserable food!" (Num 21:5). They are just days from the Promised Land and here we go again with another temper tantrum, another meltdown in the community of faith. *Then the Lord sent venomous snakes among them; they bit the people and many Israelites died (Num 21:6).* This sounds pretty harsh doesn't it? I can't believe it. Jehovah is so careful with the Edomites that he doesn't let the Israelites go that way to make sure the Edomites will be okay, and now here we are wiping out the Jews with fiery serpents. What's up with that? Does this fit your picture of the Father? Is this the Father you know? Some people see God the Father and Jesus in kind of bad cop/good cop role; don't you believe that for a second. The Father is your daddy. He's not some angry God of wrath out to get you with only Jesus to stand up for you. He's your daddy. He loves you. So what's up with these serpents? Is God really this harsh? You've got to get this now. God is so committed to our human freedom that he has elevated free choice as the highest of all universal liberties. In God's kingdom there is no greater freedom than the freedom to choose. Why? Without the freedom to choose, reciprocal love could not exist. Love must not only give you the right to say yes, but it must also give you the right to say no. If you are a young man and you have been smitten by a young girl and you go up to her and hold a gun to her head and say, "LOVE ME", I guarantee you that whatever you get from that girl, it won't be love. There is no greater freedom than the freedom to choose.

So maybe you are thinking, "But Bob, what does the Israelites' freedom to choose have to do with the venomous snakes? Surely they didn't choose those. Didn't God send the snakes to kill them?" If you look at Deut 8:15 (*He led you through the vast and dreadful desert, that thirsty and waterless land, with its venomous snakes and scorpions*), you find that the snakes have been there all along. All these years Jehovah has been leading them through this vast and terrible desert. It's a dangerous place. All these many years he has been leading them, protecting them from those fiery serpents and scorpions. He has provided water in a place where there is no water and food in a place where there is no food. These snakes were the natural inhabitants of this place. God did not suddenly create a slithering horde of snakes to punish the children of Israel – the snakes were already there. For 40 years he has been protecting this people with the shield of his presence, but it is clear that in response to the people's dark and murmuring wishes, God honors their free choice and removes himself from their presence. Why? Because God is love, and in order for it to be love, it not only must grant you the right to say yes, it must also give you the right to say no.

But doesn't it say that God "sent" the snakes? There is an important Old Testament principle that you need to keep in mind. That which God allows he is often portrayed as doing. So when the Bible says that God hardened Pharaohs heart, He simply gave Pharaoh a choice and Pharaoh decided in that moment of decision to say no to God. God didn't send the vipers. He simply stepped back. Here he said. You don't want me. I'll show you what I've been keeping from you for 40 years.

And so in this scene, God takes no for an answer and he says okay, I get it, I'm out of here. Hit the pause button here for one quiet moment. Some of you have been going through some difficult times, tough stuff. You may be tempted to just give up and kiss God off. "God I've had it with you. I begged you to save the life of my family member; I asked you to intervene and it's been like a blank wall. You've done nothing God. Adios, I'm out of here." My friend, I want you to think very carefully before you say no to

God. Do you know what he has kept you from all these years? Be careful; don't you say no on the borders of your Promised Land.

Now, evidently this land was full of these deadly snakes. Can you imagine, these Israelites are sleeping in tents - these are tents with no floors? Can you imagine, in the middle of the night these venomous vipers crawl in and looking for warmth and crawling right under the blanket with you? And this wasn't some rare occurrence. I usually sleep with one leg out of the covers, but I tucked them both in last night.

The verse says many Israelites died. *The people came to Moses and said, "We sinned when we spoke against the Lord and against you. Pray that the Lord will take the snakes away from us." So Moses prayed for the people (Numbers 21:7).* The very leader that just hours ago they had cursed, now they come to that same leader and plead with him to pray for them. Let me tell you something. I've rubbed shoulders with a few leaders over the years, and I know something. It takes a big leader to still lead the same people after he has been rejected. Here Moses immediately prays for his stricken people. The spiritual mission of a leader is to pray for his people. Moses prays for his people and God responds with this unusual three-fold instruction. *The Lord said to Moses, "Make a snake and put it up on a pole; anyone who is bitten can look at it and live." So Moses made a bronze snake and put it up on a pole. Then when anyone was bitten by a snake and looked at the bronze snake, he lived (Num 21:8-9).* Why did God have Moses make this bronze snake, put it on a pole, and then have the people who had been bitten look at it to get healed? When Moses prayed, why didn't God just heal them? Why the smoke and mirrors?

Let me tell you something about these snakes. These snakes were probably vipers. When they bite you they inject a neurotoxin into your blood that will paralyze you within seconds, and kill you within an hour or two. If you got bit by a viper, you would be paralyzed in seconds. There's no way you would be able to run to the tent of meeting and look at Moses' bronze snake on a pole. You're paralyzed. So maybe your child gets bitten - you've got two choices. You can say, "That's stupid. You don't get healed by looking at a stupid fake snake on a pole." Or you can trust God, pick up your child, and run as fast as you can to that tent of meeting. You cradle your child in your hands and point his head at that pole. Look Johnny, look at the snake! The people had rejected God and no longer put their trust in him. God's remedy required them to trust him. Your child has been bit. It's not an academic question - you don't sit and say, "Let's see now. Moses put up that brass snake and he told us what to do. Let's see, theologically, do I really think that will work?" No! Your child is dying. You pick up that child, run for that snake on a pole, and you say, "Come on Johnny. Look at it!" Do you think there was some sort of magic in that piece of twisted brass? Of course not; they knew. They knew that there was no piece of brass that would save them. They knew that only Jehovah could save them. This called for raw obedience and raw faith. "You fell by no longer placing your trust in me. Trust me now and I'll save you."

Raw faith was exactly the point Jesus was making with Nicodemus in John chapter 3. We all know John 3:16, but look at two verses before John 3:16: *Just as Moses lifted up the snake in the desert, so the Son of Man must be lifted up, that everyone who believes in him may have eternal life (John 3:14-15).*

You have to remember that the pre-incarnate Christ was with Moses in the wilderness. He is the one who came up with the divine remedy in the first place, and now he is going to explain it in a way that will shock even us. He said, "Look Nicodemus. Look at me. I am the serpent. Do you understand that?"

There must have been a gasp that sucked all the oxygen out of the room; shock on the face of that sanctimonious Rabbi. Jesus says, "I am the serpent. When I am lifted up and you look to me and put your faith in me...you live!"

Friends, the story of the serpent on the pole is much more than a snake story. God is seizing the opportunity to give the Israelites one more picture of divine redemption before they march into the Promised Land. It's much more than a snake story. You know, God loves to reveal divine truth to us using metaphors. The sacrificial lamb is a metaphor for Jesus paying the price for our sins. Numbers 21 and John 3 introduce the healing metaphor into the divine plan of salvation. While the lamb metaphor depicts the forgiveness of our sins, the serpent metaphor demonstrates the healing from our sins. It is the mysterious truth that in order to heal humanity the Savior had to become the very poison that was killing us. It's a healing metaphor. That's why physicians today have adopted the serpent on the pole as the symbol of the medical profession. You go to your doctor's office and somewhere in that office you will see the symbol of the serpent on the pole. It might be a plaque in the lobby or on the doctor's diploma, but it will be there somewhere.

When a snake bites you, the venom is called an antigen. When the antigen gets into the body, the body, if it has time, will respond to the antigen by creating anti-bodies. If you take the blood of a snake bite victim that has produced anti-bodies and extract and inject it into another person who has also been bitten, then in that other person's blood this injection of anti-bodies becomes the antidote. On the cross, an antigen was injected into Jesus. All the sins of the world, that deadly venom, that antigen, mainlined right into the heart of Jesus. At Calvary, God mainlined the antigen into his son that he might produce anti-bodies. For us, Jesus' blood becomes our antidote; all of our sins, you know, those things that you love to do but you know that God hates. Your sin – poison! Antigen, mainlined into the broken heart of the savior. If we go to the cross, if we look upon our savior and receive, we live. *Surely he took up our infirmities and carried our sorrows (poison), yet we considered him stricken by God, smitten by him, and afflicted. But he was pierced for our transgressions, he was crushed for our iniquities; the punishment that brought us peace was upon him, and by his wounds we are healed (Isa 53:4-5). He himself bore our sins in his body on the tree, so that we might die to sins and live for righteousness; by his wounds you have been healed (1 Peter 2:24).*

The metaphor of the serpent extends the power of the cross. Not only can the cross forgive our sins, it can heal us from our sins. It's mercy! What sins are there in your life that God has forgiven but that you have not yet been healed of - sins that God has forgotten but that you can't forget. The cross is the only power in the universe to heal you and me of our crippling guilt.

What is the sin that you battle with - the sins of the flesh, the sins of the mind? Pride! What's your poison? Whatever sin you struggle with today, there is an all-sufficient power at the cross to heal you. We've got to be healed; it's not enough to be forgiven. Hallelujah for forgiveness, but it's not enough. We also have to be healed. Don't die this side of the Promised Land. The healing antidote is at the cross. Look to the cross. If you will bow at the cross of Calvary, you will be healed.

CHAPTER 23

Final Failure

Moses was a man just like you and me. Some have called him the greatest leader ever born, but apart from God he was just an ordinary man whose life was filled with ups and downs, successes and failures. It was his connection to God that made him great, and he was able to accomplish great things only to the extent that he placed his trust and his life in the hands of his creator. God has created every one of us for greatness. God has a huge plan for every one of our lives. God is not a God of small plans, he only thinks big. That's why faith is so important. God is only able to accomplish his plans in us as we trust him and turn the management of our lives over to him.

Moses' life doesn't end like a Hollywood movie with the hero victorious and basking in the glory of success. In fact, the end of Moses' life serves to remind us again that Moses was not the hero of the story, but rather Jehovah, the one true God. Moses' life ends in failure, but comforted in the arms of his friend and savior. We pick up the story with the Israelites back at Kadesh Barnea, the gateway to Canaan, the land that God had promised to their father Abraham so many years ago. The last time they were here their parents didn't have enough faith to trust God to defeat the giants in the land. Now it's the kids' turn. Will they pass the test their parents failed? We pick up the story in Num 20:2: *There was no water for the congregation, and they assembled themselves against Moses and Aaron.* Can you believe it? They gathered together against Moses and Aaron. It's déjà vu all over again, again. For 40 years the children have been grumbling to Moses and Aaron. Why did you bring us here? Why don't we have any food? Why don't we have any water? Over and over again they complain to Moses and over and over again he tells him that it's not him that brought them out of Egypt, but the Lord. Now, once again they have run out of water, and once again they blame the two brothers. But this is no accidental water shortage. How do I know that? It takes two gallons of water a day to survive in the desert. That means they would need about 6 million gallons of water a day in the desert (not counting animals). There wasn't that much water in the desert. God had been supplying water all these years. It's not an accident that they ran out of water. They are getting ready to cross over into the Promised Land and this is the test to see if they are ready to go, to see if they are finally ready to trust. This is their final exam at the desert school. So God turns the water off. God tested them 40 years ago and they flunked. How will the people respond this time?

Why did you bring the Lord's community into this desert, that we and our livestock should die here? Why did you bring us up out of Egypt to this terrible place? It has no grain or figs, grapevines or pomegranates. And there is no water to drink!"(Num 20:4-5). It's you Moses!! It's you Aaron!! The people were getting ready to stone them. Apparently, the people were threatening enough that Moses and Aaron took off – *Moses and Aaron went from the assembly to the entrance to the Tent of Meeting and fell facedown, and the glory of the Lord appeared to them (Num 20:6).* I'd fall on my face too. "Dear Lord, how much of this is a man supposed to take? The kids are no better than their parents, and after all we've done for them, they are about to stone us." - Then the glory of the Lord appeared to them. God speaks – "I hear ya Moses." *The Lord said to Moses, "Take the staff, and you and your brother Aaron gather the assembly together. Speak to that rock before their eyes and it will pour out its water. You will bring water out of the rock for the community so they and their livestock can drink" (Num 20:7-8).*

Now this isn't the first time this has happened. Forty years earlier these dolts were given the same test. Actually, 40 years ago it was momma and papa who received the test. Now it's the kids being tested. When momma and papa ran out of water all those years ago, God gave Moses some instructions to try to teach faith to the people. *Then the Lord said to Moses, "Pass before the people and take with you some of the elders of Israel; and take in your hand your staff with which you struck the Nile, and go. "Behold, I will stand before you there on the rock at Horeb; and you shall strike the rock, and water will come out of it, that the people may drink." And Moses did so in the sight of the elders of Israel (Ex 17:5-6).* The Lord told Moses, "I'll be right there before you. When you strike the rock you are striking me, and I will bring water, life-giving, lifesaving water." Now that point is critical in order for us to understand what is going on in Numbers 20 with the kids. There is a dramatic piece of symbolism going on in Exodus 17, and if we don't get it we'll never understand Numbers 20. God told Moses that when he stands before the rock that it will be Christ, the pre-incarnate Christ standing there. The Apostle Paul confirms it for us in the New Testament: *...and all drank the same spiritual drink, for they were drinking from a spiritual rock which followed them; and the rock was Christ (1 Cor 10:4).* Moses was to strike the rock just as Christ was struck at Calvary. It was a powerful metaphor for the coming Messiah. It was a picture of redemption. God wasn't just testing the Israelites here in Exodus to see if they would trust him, he was also painting a living picture. It was a picture of redemption and of how the Lord would sacrifice his own son to save his people. It was the ultimate picture of God's love for his chosen. The divine command to strike the rock <u>once</u> was intended to teach Moses and Israel the truth of Calvary. *...so Christ also, having been offered once to bear the sins of many...(Heb 9:28).* The rock needed to be hit only once and for all time from Calvary's fountain life-giving, lifesaving water would flow. Jesus does not need to be sacrificed again and again and again, but once for all time. One sacrifice and the entire human race for all time is covered. "Moses, you strike that rock once. I am the rock, and when you strike me water will flow."

How radically different are God's instructions to Moses this time with his grown up children. *The Lord said to Moses, "Take the staff, and you and your brother Aaron gather the assembly together. Speak to that rock before their eyes and it will pour out its water. You will bring water out of the rock for the community so they and their livestock can drink" (Num 20:7-8).* "You don't need to strike the rock, Moses." The rock has been struck once for all time. Now you just <u>speak</u> to the rock. It's the same for us. When you sin, Jesus doesn't need to do anything more. You just cry out to him and instantly water flows, life-giving water that washes you clean.

Oh my gosh - what does Moses do? Look at verse 10: *He and Aaron gathered the assembly together in front of the rock and Moses said to them, "Listen, you rebels, must we bring you water out of this rock?"* Moses and Aaron gather everyone in front of the rock (THE Rock). Moses knows, he's been with the Rock all these years. He knows the Rock is Christ. It's supposed to be both of them speaking, but Moses jumps in..."Now listen up you rebels. Do we need to carry water for you??!! Not only did Moses lose his temper, but in verse 11 he lifts that rod up high over his head and with everything his 120 years has left, he strikes the rock. He lifts that rod and strikes it again. Moses, Moses, Moses. Even the greatest of leaders can in a moment of blinding anger spiritually melt down. Instantly God's judgment falls: *But the Lord said to Moses and Aaron, "Because you did not trust in me enough to honor me as holy in the sight of the Israelites, you will not bring this community into the land I give them" (Num 20:12).*

When I read these words, I just want to sit down and cry. My heart aches for Moses. For 40 long bone-wearying, back-breaking years he has been a nursemaid to these grown up kids. Over and over again he has pointed them to the Lord. When God got fed up with these kids and said, "I'm going to nuke them," Moses said, "No, no God! Nuke me instead. Take my name out of the book and save them." Moses has loved these grown up kids with a love that only God could have put in his heart. This is the same Moses who in one out-of-control moment, in one moment of unguarded passion, melts down in front of the whole community. The divine verdict is quick. Because you have sinned Moses, you will not cross over. You will not enter the Promised Land.

We have a heartbroken God and a heartbroken leader. What's going on? Why is God making such a big deal out of one day's meltdown? Forty years of faithfulness and one out-of-control minute. Come on God!! You forgave Aaron the golden calves. You forgave Moses the murdered Egyptian. Why can't you just forgive this time again and the story will have a happy ending. Listen; don't even think for a moment that Christ wasn't willing to forgive him. This is not a matter of forgiveness. Moses in that instant is forgiven. You say, Bob, you don't know that for sure. Yes I do. I can prove it to you. Two pages further in the book of numbers: *"He has not observed iniquity in Jacob, nor has He seen wickedness in Israel (Num 23:21).* Two pages further and God has not only forgiven, he has forgotten. Don't talk to me about God's forgiveness. You've got his forgiveness just like that! Some of you might be thinking you have screwed up royally. Your life is a mess and it's hard to imagine having hope for the future. Some of you might be dragging around a ball and chain of a memory that will not let you go and keeps you from forward progress. If you know Jesus as your Savior then Christ's character stands in place of your character and you are accepted before God just as though you had never sinned. If you don't know Jesus and you haven't received his forgiveness, then it's yours for the asking. The issue with Moses and Aaron wasn't forgiveness - the issue was leadership. You see, to whom much is given much is required. God could have said, "All the people have sinned and so nobody is going in." What did Moses do that was so bad? Why did this disobedience draw such severe judgment? By striking the rock instead of speaking to it (and by the way he strikes it twice) Moses smears God's holy Calvary metaphor. God has been painting a picture of redemption to teach the Israelites and us his plan to redeem all of mankind from the slavery and death of sin. In one out-of-control moment Moses smears the picture that God has been painting. He takes all the credit for himself by eclipsing God completely. "Must we carry water for you?" In one moment, Moses proves the people's charges that it has been Moses leading them all along, not Jehovah. Moses inadvertently puts himself in the place of God, and the judgment of God falls quickly.

What a sad story. What a sad epitaph on Moses' life. If Moses had a tombstone maybe it would read: "Here lies Moses. He sinned and didn't go in." Praise God, this isn't quite the end of the story.

Let's look at Moses' last words. The book of Deuteronomy is his farewell address to the people.

Chapter 33 contains his last words. He dies in chapter 34. For 40 years he has wept over these people. They are his kids. His last words...*Blessed are you, O Israel! Who is like you, a people saved by the Lord (Deut 33:29).*

With those last words that sagging shouldered leader climbs that mountain and everyone knows that he's not coming back. Alone, he climbs to the summit of Mount Nebo where the pre-incarnate Christ is waiting for him. "Moses, I'm here. I'm with you. I've been with you this whole time and I'm not about to leave you now. Come here Moses. Before you die I have something I want to show you. Look Moses, I'm going to give you a supernatural view of the whole Promised Land. Look, Moses, and see the whole spread. And while I'm at it, I'm going to show you the future of your people and their life in the land." Moses looks and he sees the whole sad story of disobedience and falling away over and over again, having missed the whole picture of redemption. "Oh Lord he sighs," and then Moses looks at Christ and he says, "Oh Lord, I cannot die unless I know that you have forgiven me." "You are forgiven, my friend. Now go to sleep."

Moses didn't die. The body died but Moses lives. I imagine about one millionth of a second after he fell asleep he woke up in heaven. I wonder what the first words he heard when he woke up in heaven. Maybe "Moses, welcome to the Promised Land."

Where do we fit in the story? God is doing the same thing with us today that he did back then. He tests us to see if we will trust him, and he uses our lives to paint a picture of redemption. We are His workmanship, His work of art (Eph 2:10). God is creating a picture of redemption with each of our lives. Every single one of us is to be a picture of God's love and mercy. Each one of us is to be on display as the result of Christ's sacrifice on the cross of Calvary. Maybe you say, "I'm not much of a picture. You don't know my life. You don't know the things I've done and how badly I've messed things up. There's no way that I can be a metaphor for Christ's redemptive sacrifice. I don't deserve anything but punishment and death." Well, join the club my friend. God isn't looking for clean vessels; he's looking for vessels he can clean up and teach to trust him.

When life catches up to you and you say, "I can't do it, poor me, why have all these things happened to me?" When you say, "life is hopeless", do you know what you are doing? You are saying that the cross wasn't enough. You are smearing Christ's redemption metaphor. What does Jesus want from you? He wants you to believe that his sacrifice for you is enough. He wants you not to strike the Rock, but instead to cry out to the Rock. When life happens and you cry out to Jesus, the power that God used to raise his son from the dead is instantly available to you. The Rock is Christ. Cry out to the Rock today and he will bring lifesaving, life-giving water into your life.

It's the story of Moses; It all started with the faith of one man, Moses' father, who cried out to God over concern for his unborn child and his nation. Because he believed God, both of his concerns were answered. God promised him a child that would be famous and known by all, as long as the world lasts. It's been thousands of years and every believer and every unbeliever still knows the name of Moses.

ABOUT THE AUTHOR

Bob Saffrin lives in Minneapolis Minnesota with his wife, Barb and their beagle, Rocky. They have two children and four grandchildren.   Bob has been teaching and preaching the Bible for over 35 years. You can reach Bob at bobsaffrin@gmail.com.

51738406R00102

Made in the USA
Charleston, SC
01 February 2016